INFORMATION SERVICE
IN LIBRARIES

by

D. J. FOSKETT
M.A., F.L.A.

Librarian, Institute of Education
University of London

With a Foreword by
RAYMOND SMITH, F.S.A., F.L.A.
(Formerly City Librarian
Guildhall Library)

PHILOSOPHICAL LIBRARY INC.
15 EAST 40th STREET
NEW YORK, 16, N.Y.

© CROSBY LOCKWOOD & SON LTD 1958

Published 1961, by Philosophical Library, Inc.,
15 East 40th Street, New York 16, N.Y.
Printed in Great Britain for Philosophical Library by
Fletcher and Son Ltd Norwich and
The Leighton-Straker Bookbinding Co Ltd London

Foreword by

RAYMOND SMITH, F.S.A., F.L.A.

WHEN Mr Foskett asked me to write a foreword to his book it gave me great pleasure to comply. On our first meeting, some years ago now, we discovered that we both had been studying for some time, though from different angles, the question of libraries in relation to information services. At that time Mr Foskett was directing the library and information service of a large industrial concern, while I was looking after a public reference library which catered both for historical research and for the day to day requirements of a business community. What we both had in mind was the paramount importance of libraries as sources of information, and what brought us together was an attempt to find a unity of function in libraries of all types. We wanted to satisfy ourselves that librarianship was more than a collection of techniques or a set of rhetorical platitudes. We started out not from any preconceived philosophy of librarianship or any high-flown principles but from actual practice, i.e., from observation of the constitution of libraries of all kinds in relation to the public or the clientele they served, or tried to serve. We succeeded in harmonising our conclusions to a remarkable degree and, may I say, to our own satisfaction. The impact of our discoveries on the outside world was negligible—possibly because they looked so simple and so obvious. I myself having (as I still think) found a good answer, turned to other fields of research. Mr Foskett, always the more active partner, has continued to apply his great powers of exposition and analysis, and his indomitable energy, to the consideration of the role of the library, and the librarian, in the collection, presentation and dissemination of information. As will be obvious, his thought is dominated by the basic principle we tried to establish—the unity of the profession. That unity needs not merely to be affirmed but to be demonstrated. The disciplines the profession offers need to be welded into a logical and consistent whole, and strengthened and consolidated by the assimilation of new and appropriate techniques. It is in my view the great merit of Mr Foskett's considerable achievement, that he has been able to illuminate practice by principle, and to keep a firm grasp of principle throughout the discussion of the manifold complexities of developing techniques.

9 *May*, 1958.   R.S.

Preface

ANYONE who writes a book of this sort is bound to draw heavily on the experience of others, and I have no doubt that many readers will recognize their own views and practices. Nevertheless, I have deliberately set out to give a personal view of the subject because there are already several works which cover the details much better. In particular, I would mention the Aslib *Handbook of Special Librarianship and Information Work*, *The Reference Librarian* edited by J. D. Stewart, the *Five Years' Work in Librarianship* edited by P. H. Sewell, *Library Assistance to Readers* and *Information Services* by R. L. Collison, and *Introduction to Reference Books* by A. D. Roberts. I prefer to mention these here rather than at the end of several chapters. Other references are given at the ends of chapters, but it will be obvious that these are not intended to be bibliographies of their subjects; a few footnotes have also been included.

I should like to acknowledge my debt to the many hours of discussion I have had with friends and colleagues; to Professor Raymond Irwin, Mr B. C. Vickery and Mr D. R. Jamieson, all of whom read the whole book and made many helpful suggestions; and to Raymond Smith, guide, philosopher and friend, for contributing the foreword.

D.J.F.
May 1958.

Contents

CHAPTER ONE

The Origins of Information Services in Libraries

IN a sense, libraries have always been Information Services, because the word "Information" has such a broad connotation that any person who systematically imparts knowledge to others may be called an Information Officer. That this book should begin with such an utterly commonplace observation is a measure of the futility of the years of discussion, often acrimonious, that have taken place among those who, in one way or another, build up collections of books, papers, films, gramophone records and other "documents" so that the information they contain shall be useful in circumstances other than those in which it was discovered and recorded. The youngster who left school last week helps the old gentleman to find the time of his train from Bradshaw; the scholar with research degrees draws the attention of his colleagues to newly-published work in their fields. One is at the beginning, the other at the top, of his profession, but the social role they play is the same. The nature of the information does not condition the nature of the means used to locate it, and in both cases the enquirer has first to state what he wants to know—and, sometimes, what he knows already. The social function of an information service is to find out what is known of a particular subject, and provide so much of it as is wanted by an enquirer in order to fill a gap in his knowledge.

The levels of information services, however, are very definitely conditioned by the nature of the information they deal with, and so may vary enormously. It is this fact that has led some of those engaged on the highest levels, and particularly in science, to insist that they do not belong to the same profession as librarians, who, in some libraries, may be engaged on the lowest, as well as on higher, levels. It is mainly in scientific and industrial research that the "information service" or "information library" has developed most strikingly into its present characteristic form, and the speed of this development during the last few decades is the most eloquent testimony to the abilities and success of the pioneers.

While it would be a mistake to suppose that only scientific research stands in need of information service from libraries, it was without doubt in this field that the idea originated of allotting to one individual the task of organizing the supply of newly-published information that would be useful to research workers themselves. Libraries have existed since the most ancient times; but the modern pattern of research and publication has naturally brought about changes in the pattern of the services required from them. It is not so long since a piece of research, in any field, was conceived as a whole, executed by one man, and published as an entire book. We remember that Darwin spent more than twenty years in compiling *The Origin of Species*, and, in spite of his joint paper with Wallace in 1858, no one really knew precisely, before its publication, the contents of his great work, nor the epoch-making conclusions that he drew from it. This was before the days of over-specialization, in that "healthier time", as Joseph Needham says, "when scientific books were written not for any specialized 'scientific public', but for anyone in the realm who cared to read them."[1] The first edition sold out on the day of publication.

The nineteenth century saw the beginning of many trends that have led to the present pattern of library services. Scientific experiment, in the sense of the study, however superficial, of natural phenomena, is much older than libraries, but what is characteristic of recent times is the phenomenal increase in the quantity of research, and especially its application to industry. The scientific renaissance of the sixteenth and seventeenth centuries owed something (more, perhaps, than is usually thought) to the stimulus provided by the needs of industry, for example

[1] *The Sceptical Biologist*, Chatto & Windus, 1929, p. 163.

shipping, but was largely carried on by university professors like Galileo, or wealthy gentlemen like Boyle, who had the leisure and the resources to pursue their own interests. They were willing, even eager, to exchange information with other scientists, and after personal correspondence had been the principal medium of exchange for nearly a century, the first scientific journals were founded; one or two short-lived ones preceded the first two great names, the *Journal des Sçavans* in France, and the *Philosophical Transactions of the Royal Society* in England. For the next two hundred years, books and journals continued to be published, but the number of people actually engaged in scientific research remained small, and it was customary—indeed this was expected—for a man of science to read everything in a wide field, in at least English, French and German. Many scientists were also fluent in Latin and Italian; and they probably knew personally most of those working in their field in other parts of the world.

This situation began to change during the later years of the nineteenth century, largely because of the growth of industry and the development of large-scale production and mobile labour. The history of industry is full of fascinating stories of the measures taken to guard and to steal secret processes handed down in the same works for generations, and it is said, for example, that only five people were allowed inside one of Bessemer's early factories, even though he had taken out patents on his inventions. With the introduction of machinery, the Industrial Revolution produced a new type of industry—the manufactory, where large numbers of workers were employed, any of whom might at any time desert and go to work for a competitor, taking his skill and experience with him.

At the same time, the introduction of machines brought with it the need for a technically-educated class of artisans or "tradesmen", who could work the machines, maintain them, and repair them if necessary, in numbers beyond the power of the old-established apprentice system to provide. Among the consequences of this were the Mechanics' Institutions and the Public

Libraries Act of 1850. By this time, books were recognized as sources of technical information and reference, and scientific societies were beginning to be formed and to start publishing their journals and proceedings. Agitation for technical education became general, and many great scientists, such as Davy, Faraday, Tyndall and Huxley spent much of their time giving "popular" lectures to general audiences and to "working men".

A crucial date in industrial history is 1856, when W. H. Perkin discovered mauveine, and so virtually founded the whole organic chemical industry. That he made this discovery while looking for something else, and instantly recognized its importance, emphasizes his greatness as a scientist. Now chemistry was a subject in which there was a long tradition of publication and exchange of ideas; and the rapid growth of the new industries was helped by this. Even so, the application of science to industry proceeded much more slowly in England than on the Continent; English industry prospered for other reasons. It was first in the field, it was based on some remarkable inventions, and it was able to exploit the colonial countries for cheap raw materials. It was in France and still more in Germany that the lack of these things had to be made up by scientific research.

The full effect of this was felt in 1914, when it was suddenly discovered—after war had broken out—that some vital branches of British industry, such as dyestuffs, instruments and explosives, were quite incapable of supplying the country's greatly increased demands; we had grown into the habit of importing these things, some of them from Germany itself. There was no time to build empirically, as had been customary in British industry; therefore we had to make as much use as possible of other people's knowledge.

All these developments depended more and more on the breaking down of barriers of secrecy and on free communication between research workers. The nineteenth century saw a remarkable growth of learned societies, in science and engineering, who held meetings to allow their members to benefit from each other's experience, and published journals in which papers describing new work could be given wide circulation. The ancestor of these societies, the Royal Society for the Improvement of Natural Knowledge, had already set the example two centuries before and, in the opinion of T. H. Huxley (first its Secretary, then its President),

> If all the books in the world, except the "Philosophical Transactions", were destroyed, it is safe to say that the foundations of physical science would remain unshaken, and that the vast intellectual progress of the last two centuries would be largely, though incompletely, recorded.[1]

Joseph Needham goes so far as to suggest that this free interchange of ideas is the chief characteristic of modern science:

> Is not modern science distinguished from primitive forms of science such as alchemy by the fact that the free publication of results permits of confirmation, or failure of confirmation, by a thousand observers and experimentalists, scattered over the earth's surface, of every race, religion, colour and creed? Does not science strive to perfect the means for the communicability of human thought about nature?[2]

Such a growth of publication naturally required the establishment of libraries for collection and storage, and the learned societies themselves usually formed libraries early in their histories. Libraries also began to be established by industrial firms during the century: there is a small collection in Birmingham University Library that belonged to a local iron-working firm in the early years of the century; in 1855, the *Journal of the Society of Arts* reported that the enlightened management of a New England mill had provided a library of several thousand volumes for the instruction and recreation of its workers; the I.C.I. Dyestuffs Division Library is partly based on the library built up by the firm of Levinstein Ltd. during the latter part of the century. Other firms no doubt founded libraries of which there is no

---

[1] *Collected Essays*, Macmillan, 1893. Vol. I, p. 23.
[2] *Time, the Refreshing River*, Allen & Unwin, 1943, p. 96.

record, especially in those industries most closely allied to the great societies and institutions, whose members had become accustomed to using the literature as a source of information to supplement the knowledge they had gained from their own experience.

Interest in scientific research increased rapidly during the First World War, and led to the foundation of the Department of Scientific and Industrial Research in 1916; its many research stations and the Research Associations have grown up with libraries as an important part of their work, supplying technical and scientific literature to their own scientific staff, to member firms, and in special cases to outside bodies and even individuals. The growth of this movement has been documented to some extent, but there must be a wealth of material in private and official files that could contribute to the full history of special libraries. We know that libraries existed, and were even well-established by the 1920s. Interest was shown by scientists: W. A. Barbour read a paper on "The organization of a factory library" to the Society of Chemical Industry in 1918, in which he described the Kaiser Index set up at Ardeer in 1910, for an already existing collection. E. J. Rees made a survey in South Wales which showed that several firms there were providing technical libraries for their workers, and he presented a paper on "Works lending libraries" to the Library Association Conference in 1922, urging public librarians to assist in the provision of technical literature to industry. The Proceedings of the early conferences of Aslib are full of papers describing how organizations of all kinds were collecting literature for their members, and setting up libraries to organize it.

The provision of this kind of library was not confined to organizations engaged in research in science. It was mainly in the scientific libraries, however, that a new concept of the function of a library emerged: that the library should help in the task of giving information to research workers without waiting for them to ask for it—should *disseminate* as well as *collect* information. It was

6

in the scientific libraries, in fact, that the social conditions existed pre-eminently for the development of such a function. In the first place, there was the ever-growing volume of publication, which meant that it became more and more difficult, even with increased specialization, for a research scientist to carry out his own work and at the same time read all the new publications that might contain something relevant to his work. Secondly, the very nature of scientific research makes it easier for the working scientist to derive useful assistance from someone else's study of the literature. I should certainly not wish to deny that the individual's imagination plays a vital part in the progress of science; the whole history of science contradicts such an idea, in spite of the accusations of some "Humanists" that the application of scientific method drives out the use of the imagination. Nevertheless, science does depend on the discovery of masses of facts, and not merely on flashes of inspiration; the brilliant guesses of the Greeks foundered on the rocks of their ignorance of many of the most elementary facts about natural phenomena. Now if a scientist finds, during a piece of work, that he needs to fill a gap in his knowledge, he can either carry out further work to discover the facts for himself or he can find them out from someone else. On most occasions, the second alternative recommends itself as being the easier. He may ask a colleague; he may search the literature. In either case he has to define with some precision what he wants to know, and it is no more than a step beyond this to ask someone else to search the literature for him, especially if he can ask someone who is experienced in this kind of work. A fact, so to speak, is a fact, whether I find it out for myself or learn it from another. Scientists work on this principle, and it is seen in their acceptance as fact of what is published by other scientists in the literature.

Such a sweeping statement naturally demands some reservation. No scientist of repute publishes work of whose validity he is doubtful, but we have to recognize that there are many ways of looking at the same phenomenon. So we hear now and then a warning against putting too much reliance on reading, particularly from university scientists, who are interested in training minds as well as discovering facts. The "pure" scientist, who is more concerned with the advancement of science than with the solving of specific difficulties, rightly insists that the individual must develop his own approach to his work, and not merely be content to follow in the tracks of others.[1] It is of no particular consequence if he does duplicate work already done by someone else; the experimenting itself is what is valuable, not the results alone.

The conjunction of these two factors, the great increase in the amount of publication and the character of scientific research as the discovery of facts, does not of itself bring about the intellectual climate required for the growth of information service in libraries. A very high level of scientific research has long been maintained at universities, but it was not in the university libraries that the idea of an information service emerged. Research in the university library tended to follow the pattern of research in the humanities, the librarian's principal task being to build up a collection of the best books and journals in as many subjects as possible, so that they will be available if asked for, but not to carry out bibliographical research or give an information service.

The third factor, which completed the requisite circumstances, was the widespread application of scientific research to industry. Again, there is nothing particularly new about industrial science, and J. D. Bernal has suggested that the needs of industry have been a motivating force in the progress of science for much longer than is usually thought.[2] The famous Lunar Society was founded in Birmingham in the eighteenth century; Davy made considerable investigations into agricultural chemistry, and lectured on it for the Board of Agriculture; Faraday, Perkin and Pasteur are examples of scientists whose discoveries helped to

[1] See, for example, W. I. B. Beveridge in *The Art of Scientific Investigation*, Heinemann, 1950, p. 2.

[2] *Science in History*, Watts, 1957, and *Science and Industry in the Nineteenth Century*, Routledge, 1953.

found or modernize whole industries; Huxley served for several years as a Government Inspector of Fisheries. But whereas until this century such developments had occurred somewhat sporadically, the last fifty years have brought about a complete change, so that the systematic application of science to industry is now the common pattern. Industry, which is the exploitation of natural resources for man's benefit, can profit so greatly from scientific investigations that this change was inevitable, and facilities for scientific and technical education have also greatly expanded in order to provide the necessary supply of qualified young workers.

The main difference between the academic and the industrial approach to science is that industry is mainly interested in results, in solving specific problems; in fact this is all that many firms are interested in, although a few of the largest or the highly specialized do allot some of their resources to "long-term" research. An executive of one of the biggest American firms that does this has said that he expects only 10% of his research to be commercially profitable, but that this will pay handsomely enough to make the outlay worth while.

The urge to produce results, however, means that the industrial scientist is not paid to do research to find out what is already known and published. Laboratory research being much more costly than library research, it is better to consult the literature when a new programme is being drawn up and at crucial points during the programme, in order to find out how much has already been published that will contribute to it. On the other hand, scientists are more profitably occupied at the bench than in the library, and, since books are not their primary source materials, as they are for research in the humanities, most scientists prefer to spend their time on experiments and not on reading. And the volume of publication is so great that it is impossible to do both.

All these developments led inevitably to the idea of a service of information provided by one of the staff who would be in touch with all the laboratory work, but whose primary duty would be to organize the literature—and to get to know all other possible sources of useful information. The necessity for this "Intelligence Department" was stressed by W. Rintoul, in a paper on "The control of industrial and scientific information", read to the Society of Chemical Industry in 1918; and the Research Associations began to foster the growth of information services throughout the whole of industry. The contribution of two of their directors, J. G. Pearce and R. S. Hutton, can scarcely be over-estimated.

Progress in both research and information service was slow but steady between the two world wars. The tendency was for a firm to engage first of all a works chemist, who usually brought his own books with him. When he had proved his value to the firm, other scientists were added, and properly constituted research departments formed, making their own contributions to the literature. This constant advance along the frontiers of knowledge has meant that the difficulty of making new discoveries continues to grow, until it rarely happens now that one man working on his own has the resources to carry out an extensive research programme. Not only is there a greater store of knowledge to be mastered before one comes face to face with the unknown, but the size and cost of modern equipment puts it out of reach of the private individual. Rutherford's string and sealing wax has given place to cyclotrons, synchrotrons, bevatrons and similar mammoths; the realms of supercold and superheat cannot be reached with ice blocks and bunsen burners; to launch even a football-sized satellite into outer space requires a national effort. So that while there is no doubt still a place for "string and sealing wax" (chromatography is a good example, and even this is now being developed with bigger and more complex apparatus), the characteristic pattern of contemporary scientific research is that of teamwork supported by a wealthy organization able to use the most modern techniques. Such teams are working all over the world, on similar problems, and especially in industry, where their work is directed towards the manufacture of products—

"consumer goods" and so on—which are much the same every-where: food, textiles, plastics, metal articles, and the like.

This progress from the single works chemist with his own books to the organized team engaged on large programmes has been reflected by the establishment of libraries. Where the same books and journals were required by several members of the team, the organization stood to gain by providing them itself and setting apart some space for a library to house them and look after the necessary records. Such libraries are now considered an indispensable feature of scientific research departments.

When first set up, most of these libraries fulfilled the tradi-tional role of a collecting and storing agency, but the benefit that a research team can gain from skilful use of the literature soon became obvious, as did the advantage of centralizing such opera-tions as the scanning of new literature and searching for informa-tion on specific problems. The new role for the library was based on two main requirements of its readers: the need to organize the literature to bring out its *subject* value, and the need to be kept continuously informed of newly-published work in their field, without having to ask.

I believe that it is this last factor that distinguishes the modern "information service" from any library, no matter how good, that provides information only when it is asked to do so. Much of the work of an information service is indeed done by most libraries, and, however much it may be denied, all information services are ultimately based on library methods and materials. Even the "Information Bureau" of the departmental store or the seaside resort does not have the good fortune to be staffed by persons who are omniscient. I should like to state explicitly here that I use the term "information service" in a particular sense, as I hope will be demonstrated. It may not be a very good term, and there are certainly other professional workers, such as econ-omists, who use this and similar terms for work which I should prefer to call "commercial research", and in which an informa-tion service, in what I take to be the generally accepted meaning, can certainly be a valuable part. Two recent editorials in *Nature* have used the term "Information Services" to indicate the means of publicity adopted by governments. But the origins of information services in libraries show clearly how they have come about through a set of particular conditions, and that while they no doubt existed sporadically in other types of library, it is the peculiar achievement of the scientific and industrial research library to have developed them systematically and on a large scale.

FURTHER READING

Society libraries are dealt with by K. D. C. Vernon, in "Lovely libraries: the libraries and work of some learned societies". In *Proceedings of the Annual Conference, Folkestone*, 1956. The Library Association, 1956, pp. 19-25.

W. A. Barbour: *J. Soc. Chem. Ind.*, Vol. 38, No. 3, 1919, pp. 37R-40R.

E. J. Rees: *Lib. Assoc. Record*, Vol. 24, 1922, p. 363.

W. Rintoul: *J. Soc. Chem. Ind.*, Vol. 37, No. 4, 1918, pp. 67R-68R.

A symposium on scientific information in 1918 was reported at length in the *Trans. Faraday Soc.*, Vol. 14, 1918-19, pp. 105-131.

Useful articles appear in every volume of the Proceedings of the Annual Conferences of Aslib, which has been continued as *Aslib Proceedings*.

CHAPTER TWO

The Role of the Information Officer

WHEN the need for an active service of information made itself felt, it at once became necessary to find someone to organize the service, and although the libraries had begun their existence already, they had more often than not been put in the charge of a junior member of the staff, sometimes of a typist or the secretary of the director of research. As long as the function was merely one of keeping records, it did not appear to demand qualified staff; how great a mistake this was is readily perceived by those who have to work with catalogues and indexes begun in this style. What was now required, however, was far removed from such matters as the circulation of periodical to those who asked for them, and since a good service to each individual research man depended on a good understanding of his needs, it is scarcely surprising that the position was usually assumed by a scientist already working for the organization. He would have a good scientific training, and would be thoroughly familiar with the particular research interests of his colleagues.

There is no doubt that this was justly considered to be a function of a superior order to that of the management of a small library; high qualifications were demanded of a person whom the research workers could trust not to overlook new work that might be important to them. There is obviously far more involved here than in simply building up a collection, which is bound to be small in most industrial libraries because of the limited range of subjects covered. It must be appreciated that it is no light matter for a research man to pass over to someone else the duty of keeping watch over new publications for him; nor, in fact, do they do so completely, since every scientist must read at least those that deal specifically with his own subject in his own language. S. Weinberg has pointed out that, in a small firm, the function might well be assumed by the director of research himself. He might not be aware of everything that his staff would like to read, but he would certainly know what they ought to read!

It is indeed skilled work calling for high qualifications and a clear understanding of research method. Some first class scientists have chosen information work in preference to the laboratory, and it has attractions that appeal to a certain type of mind. Nor is it any less rewarding, where the Information Officer is recognized as a senior member of the research team; he need never fear that by leaving the laboratory he is losing his chance of making a significant contribution to the progress of his firm's research. The same is true in commercial research, where vitally important work can be done in organizing information for the research staff to work on. One of the leading scientists who have assumed this function after long research experience, R. E. Fairbairn, has recently stated in a paper to the Society of Chemical Industry,

> Progressive organizations, however, are beginning to realize, more and more, that the effective utilization of existing knowledge is often comparable in value and importance with the creation of new knowledge. From my own experience formerly in research and development work and more recently in documentary work, I can say that the latter field contains many fascinating problems comparable in interest with those usually associated with research and development work.

While it is generally agreed nowadays that the information function is important, great controversy continues to rage, generating great heat but little light, over what the function actually is, and who is best fitted to perform it. Fairbairn's paper contains a brief list of tasks, but he is more concerned with problems now demanding attention than with the nature of these tasks, nor does he go beyond a rejection of the title of both "librarian" and "information officer": he writes as a chemist engaged on "the administrative work associated with the organization and dissemination of technical information". One of the more systematic attempts to define the function was made by Sir Alfred Egerton in the 1949 Aldred Lecture to the Royal Society of Arts. He followed the course of the discussions arising out of the Royal Society Scientific Information Conference of 1948, where it was agreed that special librarians and information officers should be regarded as equal in status to the research scientists who were their colleagues. Actually it is hardly surprising that the Conference reached this conclusion, since the working party that proposed it consisted mostly of special librarians and information officers.

In his Aldred Lecture, Egerton showed a diagram which illustrated his conception of an information service. It comprised three main sections:—

1. Libraries to store and supply the material.
2. Guides and arrangements of it to facilitate finding.
3. A human agency to select, evaluate and direct the material to the right reader.

To perform these tasks effectively and consistently demands subject knowledge, understanding of the needs of research workers, and skill in library techniques.

Among industrial scientists, however, there has always been a rather low opinion of the function of a "librarian", because it is thought to be exclusively concerned with the first of Egerton's three sections, which, in the industrial library, is indeed of comparatively small moment. Scientists who became information officers, therefore, sometimes claimed that in developing the active side of the service, section three, they were creating a new function; that a library, as G. A. Shires wrote, is no more than "a static service, waiting for its users to come to it". A campaign for a variously-titled Institute has been under way for some years, and has been recently revived by the overwhelming vote at the 1957 Conference of Aslib against the provision of diplomas by that body. A. Gordon Foster proposed an Institute of Documentation, for Documentation Officers, who would be assisted by

15

librarians filling the "static" function of storing and arranging material; J. E. Farradane prefers the name of Institute of Information Scientists, maintaining that it is only in science that this particular function exists.

The protagonists of this point of view base their opinions on the importance of subject knowledge for the tasks in Egerton's section three, selection, evaluation, and direction to the right reader. Now two of these form part of the established duties of librarians in other types of library, where selection is a basic necessity, and direction to the right reader is carried out at least sporadically. The controversy therefore seems to me to turn on the question of evaluation. What is meant by evaluation, and how far can anyone evaluate for a practising research worker?

The fact that we speak of a "practising scientist" or a "practising research worker" indicates that research is a sphere of activity, mental or physical, and the research worker's mastery of his subject progresses through this activity. In the final analysis, therefore, he is the only man actually able to say whether or not he already knows something newly published and, if he does not, whether it is of value to him in his work. A subject expert can from his own opinion of the value of a particular publication, and can recommend it to someone making a study of the subject; but this is not the same thing as "evaluating" for research workers. We have to remember that opinions must remain flexible at the frontiers of knowledge, and that experts in the same subject sometimes disagree—classification is a striking example of this in our own field. I doubt whether those who put so much emphasis on evaluating for the research worker would be quite so happy for someone else to evaluate for them.

We come back to the individual research worker's contribution, and it seems to me that the idea of evaluating for him is contrary to the whole spirit of research, which is that he hopes to discover something new, and so he has to organize his entire stock of knowledge towards this goal. His opinion and his use of new information cannot be determined for him by someone else

—except in so far as his superiors may decide, on grounds other than scientific, not to pursue a particular line of enquiry. He has to make his own evaluations, and these, like the discoveries he makes, must be determined by his own pattern of thought, which is unique because every individual is unique, and, given the chance, has his own unique contribution to make. University professors, and even directors of research, are often less competent than a research man, in his own field; this is, of course, one of the main reasons for employing him.

This does not mean that I dismiss altogether the notion of evaluating; on the contrary, I believe that a certain type of evaluation is characteristic of the role of the information officer. What I do not believe is that a "degree in the subject" is the only possible training for it. This type of evaluation is what one might call assigning an absolute value: deciding whether a publication is good or bad on its subject, whether it can safely be recommended to readers and included in bibliographies. This is not the same thing as deciding that this article will tell this particular scientist how to do his job and that therefore he must use it. In point of fact, this can only be done by those with *superior* knowledge, which rules out information officers for the very reason that brought them into existence: that no one nowadays has the time to read widely in the vast quantity of publications and carry on his research as well. It seems ridiculous for an information officer to claim that he has superior knowledge, in their own subjects, to those who are actually employed as specialist experts.

Evaluation, for an information officer, means knowing whether or not the new information he receives in his library is related to the work that his colleagues are doing. He may be able to suggest the nature of the relationship, but I do not see how he can expect to specify it exactly. He must be able to recognize, for example, that an article entitled "Radiation cross-linking mechanisms" may deal with the properties of polythene, and if this interests his firm he will read the article to find out. When he finds that it does, he will send it to the polymer chemist—but only the chemist can decide whether the article adds anything to his knowledge of these mechanisms. He will indeed prefer to make such a decision himself! My experience is that scientists actually fear too much evaluation, and it creates a real danger of losing their confidence; on the other hand, if they are assured that an information officer will act as a filter, and not a barrier, they will be content to rely on him to cast his net widely, on their behalf, and will value highly those pieces of information he brings them from sources they would never have had the time, or even the notion, to peruse for themselves.

It is of interest to note in this connection the practice in medical libraries. There is a number of specialized medical libraries where an information service is provided for qualified medical men. Very rarely, however, does a medical man enter library and information work, and nearly all of these libraries are staffed by qualified librarians with a wide knowledge of medical literature. The Proceedings of the First International Congress on Medical Librarianship demonstrate the high level of scholarship reached in this field.

Failure to distinguish between evaluation in the sense of knowing that particular information is sound and may be useful to one's colleagues, and telling them how to use such information, has led a few information officers to make some curious claims in the field of commercial research, in which very rapid strides have been made during recent years. Market Research itself is not a new activity, and several papers on it were read to early Aslib Conferences. But the extension of this and other kinds of economic research, budgetary control, statistical analysis, demand forecasting and so on, have led some information officers to think that all this activity comes within the scope of their "new profession"—merely because it happens to have been called information service or intelligence service, instead of a truly descriptive title such as commercial research. These claims are, of course, rejected by economists engaged in commercial research, and however much we may dislike his contemptuous attitude ("no self-respecting economist would become a librarian"), those of us who have some knowledge of this kind of work are bound to agree with the basic point of A. R. Smith.

The confusion springs from a false analogy with scientific information. The scientist derives his mastery over his subject from his laboratory work, and library materials are not his primary sources; scientific information officers, however, have the precise function of working on the literature and not in the laboratory. Commercial research contains much practical activity, such as Market Research, but much of it does depend on working with documents, which means that library materials are primary as well as secondary sources. Although this territory has been claimed on these grounds, no one has yet explained how an information officer trained in science would be able, without long experience, to evaluate commercial information and give advice to the management on such matters as the allocation of raw materials and the siting of factories.

If, however, we remain content with the function of selecting material of *possible* value, and leaving it to those employed for their specialist knowledge to decide its *actual* value to them and to the organization, we have still an important and rewarding field of endeavour which we have only begun to cultivate systematically. So far, in discussing the role of the information officer, I have concentrated almost exclusively on what is perhaps the most controversial point, but we are constantly improving well-known techniques, such as classification, or developing new ones, such as the compilation of surveys. The main difference from the traditional role of a librarian, of course, derives from the new demands for an active service and the anticipation of demands. This requires close familiarity with the needs of readers, which arise from the role that they themselves play in the business of the organization, and it seems self-evident that an information officer must be, or make himself, intimately acquainted with all the various facets of the work of those he serves. Recent history has proved, however, that this need not depend on a life-time's service with the same organization. Some of the most outstanding scientist-information officers have changed to information work on the occasion of moving to a new post.

A static service, which waits for its readers to come to it, is concerned chiefly with the administrative control of its stock; its service depends on its ability to produce specific books on request, with a minimum of delay. An information service, however, in which documents are valued for their contents and one will be as good as another if they both contain what is wanted, has to be constantly on the alert to improve its methods, which must keep pace with developments both in its organization's range of interests and in research techniques themselves. Before one can judge the efficiency of a method, however, one must first decide what it is one wants to do.

The methods of information services in libraries have tended to develop along fairly well-defined lines, which indicates that we have, at bottom, a fairly good understanding of what it is that information officers have to do. But one would not deduce this from the literature, in which great controversy has appeared, and still continues.

Since most of this argument stems from the attempts of some information officers to prove themselves superior to librarians, it may be well to recall at this point the series of stimulating talks given to the Reference and Special Libraries Section of the Library Association some years ago by Raymond Smith, then Librarian of the Guildhall. These talks were eventually summarized in a conference Paper, and their thesis was that libraries of all types come into existence as parts of organizations, and that their function is to implement the policy of their organizations by means of books and other recorded data. Raymond Smith showed with great clarity how such a conception of a library's social role as a basis indicates the role of its staff and the type of qualification they require to carry it out, and this conception applies as much to industrial information services as to university and public libraries.

There are obvious differences in the type and level of the materials handled, and sometimes in the purposes for which they are used. Fundamentally, however, the nature of the various services provided is the same, and they may be divided into two main groups: (1) those which arise from the demand from readers to be kept informed of newly-published work, and (2) those which arise from the need to supply information on specific points when requested—what is sometimes called retrospective searching. These services may take many forms and often reach the highest levels of scholarship; and it is my opinion that the information officer who organizes and performs them has taken librarianship to its most advanced state, but has not founded a new and qualitatively distinct profession.

FURTHER READING

S. Weinberg: *Aslib Proc.*, Vol. 3, No. 1, 1951, pp. 22-29.

R. E. Fairbairn: *Chemistry and Industry*, May 25, 1957, p. 645.

G. A. Shires: *Trans. Inst. Rubber Ind.*, Vol. 24, No. 3, 1948, p. 120.

Sir Alfred Egerton: *J. Roy Soc. Arts*, No. 4800, 1949, pp. 680-704.

Proceedings of the First International Conference on Medical Librarianship, edited by F. N. L. Poynter. *Libri*, Vol. 3, 1954—the whole volume is given to these proceedings.

A. R. Smith: *Aslib Proc.*, Vol. 6, No. 3, 1954, pp. 159-168, and Vol. 8, No. 4, 1956, pp. 252-265.

D. J. Foskett: I have discussed the relation of library to readers in "Readers' needs in the industrial library", *Lib. Assoc. Record*, Vol. 59, No. 11, 1957, pp. 353-359.

The talks by Raymond Smith were summarized in a paper in *Proceedings of the Annual Conference, Hastings* 1954. The Library Association, 1956, pp. 22-29.

CHAPTER THREE

Selection and Acquisition of Stock

IN a careful analysis of the use of staff in the small information library, B. C. Vickery linked the selection of stock to the administrative control of the whole library: "whoever has the responsibility of selecting items for purchase ... should be ultimately responsible for the rest of the library work. He holds the key in his hands—the book stock, upon which all library activity is founded." This emphasizes the importance of selection, and is probably true for any library. It does not mean, of course, that only the head of the library may select, but that he should approve all purchases and be able to justify them. He may have to work through a Library Committee, which has its advantages as well as its disadvantages but is not usual now; but he will certainly be wise to enlist the help, on an informal basis, of the experts in the various subjects he has to cover. They are usually eager to help—in fact they may become too eager, and offer suggestions for more than the library really needs in their particular fields. But to obtain books on approval and consult the expert is a very sound procedure for two main reasons: it secures good advice on selection, and ensures that the expert sees the newest books on his subject.

First of all, however, it is necessary to be quite clear about the principles on which stock is selected for the information library, and an excellent exposition of them has been given by D. V. Arnold. He stresses the need for knowing the interests of the organization and of the individual research workers in it, because it is to serve these that the library exists. The important thing is that one must have access, in one form or another, to all the work being done in those fields that relate to the organization's own research.

This is very much more difficult than appears at first sight. It has been suggested that the problems of selection found in large general libraries are not met with in the specialist library, simply because of this necessity to know of *all* relevant research; and indeed, the main problem is not that of making a choice of those books on which the book fund would best be spent, and going without the others. Even if a new work costs several pounds (as it usually does nowadays), the criterion is still, "Can we afford to be without it?" rather than "Can we afford it?" Special libraries do not, as a rule, buy books simply because they are nice to have, but books that will save a research man's time to an extent greater than their cost. This principle involves something like complete coverage of those fields in which the organization has a continuous interest. It may also justify the *exclusion* of certain works, such as multi-volume encyclopedias, that librarians tend to regard as essential in any library. Coverage in marginal fields, as Arnold points out, can be worked out on a co-operative basis; and there are numerous co-operative schemes in operation, some on a subject and national basis, such as the Research Associations, and some on a general and local basis, such as the Sheffield, Liverpool and West London (Cicris) schemes. Coverage in fields of temporary interest may also be based on co-operation, but temporary interests are often acute and may be better served by purchase.

The main problem, however (and this may be of less importance in the general library), is actually to find out the existence of new publications. Although we no doubt have better bibliographical control than has ever existed before, it is still surprising how often a useful paper is picked up only some years after its first appearance. To-day, the vast apparatus of publishing and recording seems almost stultifyingly complete, and it is only when one examines a subject field in detail that one realizes how haphazard and ill-organized is the machinery for recording new work.

One of the best methods of obtaining regular information

about new books is to make one's interests known to publishers and booksellers, many of whom circulate lists and prospectuses, often in advance of publication. Seeing travellers can be dismissed at once as being far too time-consuming. The accessions lists of libraries specializing in similar fields are valuable, particularly if the library is large or known to be collecting systematically in particular subjects. The national bibliographies that have been established in several countries obviously give the best coverage for their own books, and the *British National Bibliography* has proved how useful such a tool can be even to the highly-specialized library; and as more research organizations begin to deposit their publications at the British Museum for listing, the value of the *B.N.B.* increases.

It is well known, in fact, that it is not difficult to get to know about newly-published books. The periodical article, the short pamphlet, even advertising material, now form the characteristic media through which research workers publish, and it would be impossible to give even the most incomplete list of such publications here. What may be useful is some account of the types of organization where original work is carried on, and of the types of publication by means of which it is circulated. Most of my examples are taken from the world of scientific research, partly because it is the one I know best, and partly because it is probably the most highly organized.

The largest amount of research is done in most countries nowadays by the Government; in fact, it is estimated that more research is done by the U.S. Government than by any other organization. In this country, the Government carries on scientific research through several largely autonomous bodies: the Services and their Ministries, the technical Ministries such as Supply, Agriculture, Fisheries and Food, and Local Government, the Medical and Agricultural Research Councils, and the Department of Scientific and Industrial Research. The D.S.I.R. itself operates in two main ways: it acts through its own research stations, which are concerned with fields of national interest, such as the National Physical Laboratory and the Geological Survey, and it helps to finance the semi-autonomous Research Associations, which now cover most of our important industries. Private firms contribute part of Research Association finances, and also co-operate in running Development Associations, which do research to promote the use of a particular product—for example the Aluminium Development Association and the Timber Development Association. Industry also, of course, carries on its own research, mostly in the larger firms and in the more scientific industries; there are many well-known products on the market to-day that had their origin in a research laboratory. Polythene is a good example of a product with certain outstanding properties that was discovered by accident, as it were, while the scientists were actually studying the effects of very high pressures on various materials. Finally, there is the traditional home of research, the Universities, which have also set up some departments of applied science, such as the Long Ashton Department of Agricultural and Horticultural Research at Bristol, the Department of Textile Technology at Leeds, and the Department of Glass Technology at Sheffield, set up as long ago as 1914.

These have their parallels in other countries and reflect, as one would expect, the prevailing interests. Germany is again strong in chemistry and physics; in France viticulture and enology are studied in research stations and in University schools that are world-famous; Universities in the United States offer degrees in almost every trade activity, and their schools of business management are outstanding. Research in the humanities and in the social sciences is also carried on in many specialized institutes as well as in university departments themselves.

All these organizations publish the results of research work, through various channels, of which the most important for the research library is the periodical. It is often said that the reason why research workers publish in periodicals is the delay in producing books, but this is not the whole of the story. Some journals, especially the very best, have publishing delays even longer than those of books. The real reason is that in research work nowadays discoveries are often made in little bits much more fittingly published as periodical articles. A special form of periodical is the abstracting journal, and librarians ought to be familiar with as many of these as possible, because they are the most important reference tools in research, especially in science. Their value is shown by the fact that they are increasingly coming into use in the social sciences and the humanities also. Unesco has played a very valuable role in the promotion of abstracting, and of documentation in general, in these fields.

A type of publication serving a similar purpose is the annual review of a subject. These are now published in many fields. Perhaps the best known are the *Annual Reviews* published by Annual Reviews Incorporated, which have been established for some years; in this country we also have many, for example the *Applied Chemistry Reports*, the *Year's Work in English Studies*, and so on.

Periodicals may be published by many different organizations, though the most valuable are, on the whole, those published by societies and institutions. The American Chemical Society, for example, publishes the *Journal of the American Chemical Society*, *Industrial and Engineering Chemistry*, *Analytical Chemistry*, *Journal of Physical Chemistry*, *Journal of Organic Chemistry*, *Chemical and Engineering News*, and, last but by no means least, *Chemical Abstracts*. Very many societies and institutions publish journals which are similarly regarded as the leading records of research in their fields. The periodicals published by trade firms vary greatly in quality, with some outstanding ones like *Nature*, *Discovery*, *The Economist*, and *The Connoisseur*.

In addition to periodicals, books and pamphlets, there are two other classes of material that are important in scientific research: specifications and trade literature. Specifications are particularly important, because they either set a standard of quality which a product should reach, as in those of the British Standards Institution and similar national bodies in other countries, or they contain a complete description of an invention, as in patents. Their importance for the research librarian is obvious, and he must always ensure that his readers know about them, or they may produce something that is substandard, or an infringement of somebody's patent rights, and so become involved in unpleasant correspondence and even lawsuits. Trade catalogues are valuable because very often they give the fullest available description of a product, and frequently contain a great deal of scientific information that is nowhere else so conveniently assembled and attractively presented. It must be remembered, however, that trade literature serves a very particular purpose—to sell things; and the writers of it usually take an optimistic view of their products. They may be, and sometimes are, quite justified in doing so; but the fact should be borne in mind by librarians looking for the answer to an enquiry.

Libraries that collect only books and pamphlets, or items that begin their lives as separate, individual objects, may be satisfactorily stocked by checking bibliographies and lists of various kinds for new titles. Most libraries to-day, even the smallest and most backward, are obliged to look farther afield in order to cope with the specialized enquiries that arise out of the increasing complexity of our social life. This is particularly true of research libraries, in all fields; in the first place, their chief function is to answer enquiries on specialized subjects, and in the second, the piecemeal publication of research results makes them chiefly dependent on periodical literature. Again, where, as in scientific research, the object of an information service is to give research workers literature that will save them having to do the work themselves, the librarian's net must be cast as widely as possible, and he has to provide other services, such as photo-copying and translation, that enable him to give his readers their material in a form in which they can use it.

The objective to be aimed at is thus to see everything; and although this is probably impossible for any library whatever, it is nevertheless important to remember that it is the objective, since this provides the driving force to ensure that nothing is overlooked, that all sources *must* be checked. The librarian must pursue his quarry relentlessly, only leaving the bibliographical trail when he is convinced that it has petered out and has not merely become temporarily obscured.

Such intensive searching cannot be undertaken without a high proportion of staff to stock—which is another reason why information service has been chiefly developed in research libraries of comparatively small size. In the beginning of such a library, advice on what stock to buy would be best obtained from the various specialists, who know at least the more important works in their own fields. Thenceforward, the librarian should examine, as closely as time allows, every new publication to reach him. This can result in an enormous amount of work: even the stoutest and most devoted heart would quail at the thought of checking the enormous bibliographies appended to some modern research publications, particularly German and American. Indeed, it is well known that some of these are no more than immense surveys of the literature, and while they may be invaluable when working on a particular enquiry, they cannot be considered as useful sources of current information in a bibliographical sense.

All new periodicals should be scanned on arrival, and it is customary nowadays for the librarian to be first on any circulation list. This serves several purposes: it gives him the opportunity to look at the review columns and "Books received", and it also enables him to keep right up-to-date in his subjects and to mark forward any items of special interest to his colleagues. Naturally, there is a limit to the number of periodicals that one librarian can satisfactorily deal with in any detail, though so far as I know no one has yet made an estimate of what it is. I have found that above about 250 titles one lands in the region where one begins to skip the less interesting journals.

Many information libraries do in fact subscribe to more titles than this; and if the scanning is to be done thoroughly, it must be shared. If possible, the work should be done by other members of the library staff, senior people who are able to bring to bear the same sort of sensitivity to items of interest as the librarian himself. This can only be developed by experience; one learns by practice how to look at each page of a journal, picking out those items that need closer attention. If the sharing has to be done with members of the research staff, they will certainly need to be tactfully trained to look at their journals with the eyes of the whole department and not only their own. Nevertheless, this is done successfully in many research organizations, and it has the advantage of making the staff read the new journals quickly, so keeping themselves well-informed. Sometimes, this practice is linked with that of requiring the research staff to produce abstracts for the library bulletin.

Journals that contain abstracts should certainly be scanned by the library staff. This is not the most attractive part of a librarian's life, because the average abstract is a very dry and parched specimen; one Research Association, in fact, advises its members not to read the abstracts through from cover to cover, because "it takes a long time and makes dull reading". Scientists and other specialists are accustomed, more or less, to using them, and are willing to put up with the presentation for the sake of the matter, but if the library subscribes to very many, searching them may become a somewhat tedious business. What compensation there may be lies in the joy of the bibliographical hunt, the chance of discovering an important new paper or an interesting piece of information relevant to some part of the research programme.

It must be said here that better co-ordination among abstracting journals will have to be brought about before long. Every one I know grows bigger every year, and if the index to *Chemical Abstracts* for 1947-1956 occupies 19 large volumes and costs hundreds of dollars, where will such growth end? One can have nothing but admiration for the achievement of the editor, Dr E. J. Crane, who has reared a monument more enduring than bronze if anyone has, but if this dedicated search for completeness puts the journal out of reach of all but a few subscribers, has it not defeated its own ends? The important thing, however, is not mere size; as more and more papers are published, abstracting journals are bound to grow bigger, and this, being a reflection of the progress of research itself, is highly desirable. The important thing to consider here is that there is so much duplication; we are obliged to pay over and over again for abstracts of the same papers (sometimes of little value in the first place), issued by societies, professional institutes, research associations and so on. The reason always given by these publishers is that they abstract each paper for a particular set of readers—their own members or subscribers—whose needs are not the same as those of the other publications. There is no doubt some truth in this, even if a considerable proportion of each group of subscribers consists of the same people; but when one faces the resulting increases in costs and labour, one cannot escape the feeling that sooner or later this consideration must give way to the greater need for co-ordination and economy.

Just as the library needs a simple but efficient routine for purchase, so it also needs a similar routine for obtaining papers picked up from abstracting journals and similar sources. The usual procedure is to borrow the item first, so as to have the chance of examining it before deciding whether or not to purchase, but it should always be remembered that it may be cheaper to buy a copy (of a cheap pamphlet or short article for example), even if it turns out to be of no value, than to borrow it from another library. Borrowing undoubtedly costs more than appears at first sight, even if the high "average" figures given by some so-called authoritative sources are quite misleading—as is becoming generally recognized.

Selection and acquisition of foreign material presents several problems. The two most important are: finding out the existence of the work, and being able to obtain it when discovered. Both of these difficulties have been greatly lessened during recent years, and are being studied by committees of librarians at present.

Finding out the existence of a new paper or book in a foreign language is becoming easier because most countries where research results are published are now attempting to produce systematic records of these publications, in the form of national bibliographies and abstracting or indexing journals covering various subject fields. Publishers themselves are more willing to send their catalogues to our libraries, and it is always worth writing to a foreign publisher known to specialize, even if only to a limited extent, in one's own fields. Many American books are now listed in the *British National Bibliography*, whose policy is now to include all books handled in this country by a single agent. The publication of national bibliographies is being encouraged by Unesco, and while it would probably be out of the question for the average special library to subscribe to them, they are received by some of the large general libraries, where they can be consulted. And some foreign publishers adopt the useful practice of sending their books to the British specialized journals for review; this means waiting, of course, but it has the great advantage of bringing expert opinion as well as the notice of the book.

Important foreign periodicals are now being covered in greater numbers by English-language abstracting and indexing services. *Chemical Abstracts* is, of course, famous for its international scope, and in 1956 increased its coverage of Russian journals immensely by using abstracts published in the *Referativny Zhurnal*. Several of the Research Associations include foreign books and papers in their abstracting journals, and there are several international periodicals, like the *Review of Documentation*, that publish selected abstracts from the literature of many different countries. The various indexes of the H. W. Wilson Co. of New York also cover some important foreign journals, but as their criterion for inclusion is primarily a commercial one, their selection is not necessarily the most useful for British libraries. The *Industrial Arts Index* and the *Education Index*, for example, both show an unnatural deficiency of British journals. It may be said without fear of contradiction, however, that efficient abstracting and indexing journals are of value to librarians for current selection as well as for retrospective searching, and that no special library can be regarded as satisfactory without those that cover its special fields of interest.

Obtaining the items when discovered may be a difficult matter for "non-library" reasons, of which the most frustrating are currency regulations and the inefficiency of booksellers. Once again, steps are being taken to remedy the situation. Many British booksellers have obtained import licences and have appointed agents abroad, while undertakings such as the Farmington Plan have done a lot to make foreign booksellers conscious of the need for wide publicity for their goods. Perhaps a more important problem is the difficulty—at times the impossibility—of examining a foreign book before deciding whether or not to purchase. As might be expected, this applies particularly to specialized books, of which British booksellers are chary of stocking copies because of the limited demand. This difficulty does not apply to periodicals, since most of their publishers will supply a specimen of two on request.

This brings us to the matter of national coverage of foreign material, which is now being examined by a committee of the Library Association. I should not like to generalize about this, but a detailed examination of one field of technology shows beyond doubt that foreign periodicals are much easier to find in this country than foreign books. The titles of periodicals, moreover, are likely to be quoted sooner or later in the abstracting journals, but it seems that many books, in this particular technology at least, are not indexed or reviewed anywhere. As Arnold says, there is a very great need for more international subject bibliographies and directories of research organizations.

One of the simplest ways of acquiring some forms of material, and especially foreign material, is by exchange, and this is now widely practised by libraries of all types. It is, of course, characteristic of special libraries that they should be able to do this on a large scale, for most of them produce bulletins of one sort or another to disseminate the information they receive. As has often been observed, exchange is perhaps the best way of all of acquiring Russian, Chinese and East European publications, and libraries in those countries are usually given quite a range of publications to offer. Another very useful source of research papers is the authors themselves, who often receive reprints for distribution. Libraries should apply to authors only as a last resort, because they receive only a few reprints free, and have to pay for extra copies. They may be willing to exchange, however, and contacts made in this way can lead to useful collaboration and further exchanges of information.

Finally, there are the organizations specifically set up for the purpose of making exchanging systematic. The British National Book Centre is probably the best known in this country, and has been described in several articles. The Library Association's Medical Section has been organizing a periodicals exchange scheme for several years, with headquarters at the Wellcome Historical Medical Library; and it is possible, if rather complicated, to exchange duplicates with American libraries through the United States Book Exchange, situated at the Library of Congress in Washington.

It is clear that there can be no simple formula for obtaining and registering all the many and various types of documents received in information libraries. The simple practice of sending a marked copy of the *British National Bibliography* to a local bookseller may be a cause for envy, but hardly for imitation. All kinds of record have been advocated, but there is as yet no universally accepted system, and a neat piece of research on the matter might well be undertaken. In the meantime, each library has to make its own arrangements; we can only bear in mind the maxim that the number of records should be an irreducible minimum, and that records that are only required temporarily can easily do duty for more than one purpose. The proliferation of unnecessary records is one of the simplest ways of wasting staff time that can be found.

FURTHER READING

B. C. Vickery: *Aslib Proc.*, Vol. 3, No. 4, 1951, pp. 223-233.

D. V. Arnold: *Bibliography and book stock*. Library Association, London and Home Counties Branch, 1954, pp. 19-24.

A recent book describing the publishing organizations is *The organization of science in England*, by D. S. L. Cardwell, Heinemann 1957.

Trade literature is discussed by Eric Simons in *Manchester Review*, Vol. 5, 1949-50, pp. 351-358.

Two papers on foreign material were given by E. A. Baker and A. J. Walford in *Reference and Special Libraries: some current problems*. Library Association, R.S.L. Section 1955.

Several articles on the Farmington Plan are indexed in *Library Science Abstracts*.

CHAPTER FOUR

Arrangement and Indexing

WHILE the systematic arrangement of a library's stock has long been admitted to be one of the most important foundations of its work, there is a most significant and revealing difference in the attitude towards classification shown by public librarians on the one hand and librarians of other types of library on the other. This also seems to be true of librarians in the U.S.A. In no other sphere, perhaps, does the difference mirror so clearly the difference in attitude towards library service as a whole. Most public librarians, committed to the antiquated and now grossly inefficient Decimal Classification, are content to cramp and confine all new knowledge in this straitjacket, regardless of the inconvenience and frustration of their readers. They have used their influence to shackle the *British National Bibliography*, and, what is perhaps more important to the rest of us, they actively resist any attempt to change this state of affairs and bring this part of the national library service more into line with modern thought. Fortunately, the Schools of Librarianship now possess some first-class teachers, so that the new generation of young librarians is being taught to appreciate that classification is a means to assist reference service, and not some sacred cow to be kept alive by periodical *ex cathedra* revisions from the office in the Library of Congress.

University librarians have at least shown their awareness of modern thought, and several have adopted either the Library of Congress Classification or Bliss's Bibliographic Classification; they have not shirked the of task re-classifying even hundreds of thousands of volumes in order to make their arrangement more up-to-date.

Even special librarians have to some extent held up progress by their widespread adoption of the Universal Decimal Classification, which is now backed by the British Standards Institution. But the continuous discussion and research carried on by special librarians and information officers show their dissatisfaction with the present situation, and it is from among them that the Classification Research Group, one of the most active groups in the whole field of librarianship, draws its members. The reason is simple: it is in the information library that reference service is most highly developed, and consequently the lack of a good modern system of arrangement most keenly felt.

The placing of books in order on the library shelves is only the beginning of the function of a classification system, though it has occupied an important place in the literature of the subject. This is partly because it was the first function to be defined, and partly because the mere number of books to be classified keeps it constantly before us. Neither of these two reasons carries much weight in the special library, where all kinds of documents are collected for the information they contain, and where a scrap of paper recording a telephone conversation may well be more important than the most modern textbook. The term "information retrieval" is in fact truly descriptive, and is being widely adopted in spite of receiving its share of criticism from those who are unwilling or unable to recognize its true significance. It is because the general schemes are so hopelessly unable to cope with the *minutiae* of the special library that so much thought and research have gone into the quest for a new scheme.

Until this century, library classifications were "enumerative", in the sense that they consisted of enormously long lists of subjects; the compilers' object was to enumerate every subject on which books might be written, arranging their lists in sequences said to be derived by a process of Aristotelian logic. This process had proved very valuable in the classificatory sciences, where the grouping of objects that displayed various degrees of similarity enabled them to be studied more systematically than ever before. This type of classification, however, cannot do more than list the names of things—nor, in fact, has more than this been attempted in the classificatory sciences. But the subjects of modern research publications are far more than mere descriptions of objects, and the need has long been felt for a system that would provide a much higher degree of expressiveness, and in particular would be able to arrange not only specific subjects, but subjects in relation to one another.

While this was vaguely recognized already in the Decimal Classification when it began to use the Geography schedules for subdividing other subjects, the first general scheme to use the method of "assembling" parts of a complex subject was the Subject Classification of J. D. Brown. This scheme had a certain popularity in British libraries, but was being abandoned already in 1939, when the third edition appeared. Brown allowed for assembly, or synthesis as it has come to be called, by providing a separate table, the Categorical Table, which listed aspects and attributes that might apply to several of the subjects listed in the schedules themselves.

The UDC and the BC have both used this method so that the various parts of complex subjects may be collected from different parts of the scheme. But, like SC, they are both basically enumerative in that they set out to list, in each class, as many subjects as possible. It was not until S. R. Ranganathan began to write that the theoretical basis of the synthetic method was fully explored. His Colon Classification (which is not a particularly good example of his theories!) was first published in 1933, and he has explained how at that time he was not fully conscious of the principle he was using, that of "facet analysis".

There can be no doubt that this technique, which consists of itemizing each aspect or "facet" of a subject, must be the basis of future schemes of library classification. An examination by Vickery of modern trends in research into the subject shows how schools of thought which begin with widely differing premises are beginning to arrive at similar conclusions: that instead of starting with arbitrarily chosen main classes which are conventionally

37

agreed subjects ("physics", "economics", "history" and so on), and dividing them into more and more specific subjects by the rules of logic, we have to start with categories of things that bear some recognizable relation to each other in particular contexts.

The major function of library classification in information retrieval is that of presenting to the reader a detailed map or picture of his subject. Since the enquirer is trying to find information that he does not already know, the chances are that he will not be able to formulate his requirements precisely. A really helpful sequence of documents (which may be books, pamphlets or index cards) will lead him on from territory that he recognizes to what is still unknown to him. The closer the pattern of the scheme approaches the pattern existing in the real world—the "order of nature"—the more helpful it will be. All the arguments about distinctions between philosophical, scientific and "practical" library classifications are reduced to mere words by this simple fact.

The real world consists of matter and processes; no part of it exists in isolation, but all the parts are liable to interpenetrate, influence and change the others. When such phenomena are studied, they are written about, and it is this record that the librarian has to classify—to put it into such a place in his library that it will be discovered, or "retrieved", by those who are also studying the same phenomena.

Only a truly faceted classification provides the means for doing this, and most modern special systems have used the method, even if not consciously—as appears to be the case with the ASM-SLA Classification for Metallurgical Literature, to judge by its inconsistencies. The same sort of method, in fact, was used by Kaiser in the Ardeer index as long ago as 1910: he related Concretes and Processes, with Higher Collectives and Lower Specifics to show upper and lower genus-species relationships. He did not publish a scheme of classification based on this method, however.

The Colon Classification itself does not, unluckily, provide much encouragement to experiment with it. Being based on "literary warrant"—contrary to what ill-informed opinion has proclaimed since 1933—it is incomplete in just those parts in which the literature to be found in India is incomplete: in science, but more especially in technology. And it is precisely in libraries in these fields that the need for a good, flexible scheme is most keenly felt.

However, thanks to the power of the method, it is a comparatively simple matter to make a faceted classification—nothing like the labour involved in making an enumerative scheme, because one does not have to make a list of all the possible subjects of documents, such as "the canning of fruit and vegetables", "the freezing of fish", "the meat-packing industry". All that is needed is a list of the component terms that may occur in each of the facets of these subjects; these terms can then be combined as required by the literature.

The first step in making a faceted scheme, therefore, is to examine the literature of the subject to be classified. In Food Technology, we get subjects like those quoted above, and it soon becomes clear that we need two main lists of terms, or facets: one for Products (fruit and vegetables, dairy products, cereals, fish, meat, etc.), and one for Processes (canning, freezing, dehydration, etc.). These facets are completed as far as possible, and the best way of doing this is to take some encyclopedic survey of the subject, or the nearest approach to one, and ensure that no Product or Process mentioned in it has been left out of its appropriate facet. In Food Technology, we derive the Product facet:

> Foodstuffs, general
> > Dairy products
> > Sugar and sugar confectionery
> > Cereals and cereal products
> > Bakery products
> > Edible oils and fats

Fruit and vegetables
Meat and meat products
Fish and fish products
Flavourings
Additives
Beverages, general

Each of these headings may be further subdivided. For example:

Sugar and sugar confectionery
Sugars
Manufactured sugars
Syrups
Molasses
Treacle
Honey products
Sugar confectionery, sweets
Starches, starch products

The main headings in the Operations or Processes facet may be obtained from a similar source, but for the subdivisions of each heading it will probably be necessary to go to a textbook dealing in detail with the Product. This is, I think, true of all technologies, and may well be true in other fields: that a first facet whose contents are all related to each other by being collateral species of the same class may produce a second facet composed of groups of terms not necessarily related to each other; but each group is related to one term, and one only sometimes, in the first facet. There will, as a rule, be only a few sub-divisions of the Operations facet that could apply to all the terms in the Products facet. In Food Technology, we have instances of both. The Operations facet is as follows:

Preliminaries, preparation
Processing
Preserving
Semi-preserving

> Packing, despatch
> Storage
> Testing

Some of the subdivisions of each of these headings can apply to several products, and some to only one: the operation "peeling", for example, applies to fruits but not to milk.

A set of coding symbols, the notation, has to be added to each term in order to mechanize the arrangement of documents classified by the scheme. To classify, the appropriate terms are selected from the various facets represented in the subject of the document, and their notations joined together.

The two systems of notation are given to show that the type of notation has no influence on the method of procedure.

Examples:—

(1)	F53	Foodstuffs, general (Products facet)	Kb
	39	Preserving, irradiation (Operations facet)	Lex
	:	(joining symbol)	none

Subject: Food preservation by irradiation F53:39 or KbLex

| (2) | F5341 | Bread | Kfb |
| | 332 | Canning | Lef |

Subject: Canning of bread F5341:332 or KfbLef

| (3) | F53133 | Milk powder | Kck |
| | 7112 | Gas packing with carbon dioxide | Llf |

Subject: Gas packing of milk powder with carbon dioxide F53133:7112 or KckLlf

One proceeds further as the literature demands. An article on "the production of concentrated orange juice from Seville oranges" shows the need for a Parts facet and a Raw Materials facet, to list such things as "juice" and "Seville oranges". Similarly, "the spoilage of canned raspberries by *Byssochlamys fulva*" shows the need for an Agent or Tool facet, to list spoilage organisms and so on.

This brings us to the question of the relation between a general and a special classification scheme. The Raw Materials in Food Technology are the Products in Farming, and in the scheme quoted above, which is an expansion of CC Class F53, the Raw Material facet is copied from the Products facet in the classes Agriculture and Animal Husbandry. Causes of spoilage can likewise be copied from other classes, according to the nature of the cause: physical, chemical, microbiological. Sooner or later, anyone making a special scheme comes up against this problem, and this, being one of the most awkward parts of making the scheme, constitutes the strongest and most pressing argument for the construction of a new general scheme. Obviously, it would have to be based on a number of special schemes; but it needs to be an integration, and not merely an aggregation, of them. One problem not yet solved is the selection of "main classes" to start on, but both Vickery and Farradane have given some thought to this matter. Farradane's system of isolates and analets, that is of building up classes from individual items, is now well known. He examines the literature, constructs analets for the documents by joining isolates together with signs called "operators", and builds up his facets by making lists of isolates that have a class relation to each other.

An outstanding event in classification has been the publication of the *British Catalogue of Music*. This quarterly catalogue of all new British music and books on music is arranged by a new scheme of classification drawn up by E. J. Coates, chief subject cataloguer of the *British National Bibliography* and one of the foremost members of the Classification Research Group. The scheme has a faceted structure, and was compiled in consultation with leading musicians and music librarians. So far, it is working well, and it will be a pilot project for a new general scheme; already some public libraries have decided to change their music collections to the new arrangement, and the experience thus gained will be a very valuable guide in future changes.

Library classification schemes are all more or less systematic arrangements of subjects, the assumption being that readers are interested in subjects primarily; and certainly nearly all readers do approach libraries, particularly special libraries, to find information on subjects. It must not be forgotten, however, that certain classes of material need special attention, either because their arrangement by subject brings its own problems, for example pamphlets and works in distinctive series, or because the reader's approach is not usually via the subject, even though it is the subject content of the material that interests him. Patent and standard specifications, and Statutory Instruments, are examples of documents usually asked for by their number; trade catalogues by the name of the firm issuing them. No hard and fast rule (except that of helpfulness to the reader) can be given, because all these documents are often sought by subject too, and because in a subject search it is vital to pick up such material; in industry it can easily turn out to be the most important of all.

We can deduce from this one rule, however, which is already widely observed, but of which the importance can hardly be exaggerated. It is that, as far as is economically feasible, all the possible approaches of readers to their material must be catered for. A library classified by subject must have an author and subject index, a statement which seems obvious; but it is surprising how many people forget that author and subject indexes form essential parts of a classified catalogue also, and are not merely additional elaboration.

By some process shrouded in obscurity, the terms "catalogue" and "index" have come to be used with almost the same meaning but applied to different classes of materials. We usually refer to the "catalogue" of books, and the "index" of periodical articles. Pamphlets and leaflets form an uncommitted class, and in some libraries may be found in both the catalogue and the index!

The principal functions of catalogues and indexes are to act as records of possession and as guides to location. While catalogues on cards are no doubt most widely found, many special libraries have printed the catalogues of at least their books, and the printed form is far and away the most convenient and acceptable to the reader. A library that can afford to print its catalogue is certain to increase the use of its stock, because the record is placed in the reader's hand in a form that encourages him to use it. No one really enjoys browsing through a card or even a sheaf catalogue, whereas a printed volume, whether it be a handy pamphlet or as large as the catalogue of the London Library, invites consultation. Indeed, the very existence of such enormous books as the U.S. Catalogues fascinates many readers, and I am certain that to provide a printed catalogue removes one of the many psychological barriers erected by librarians (and usually invisible to them) between readers and their books. A useful piece of research could be undertaken on modern methods of reproducing catalogues, so as to provide a cheap and quick apparatus, and so make it possible for any library to print.

It is sometimes said that the sequence of cards in the catalogue should not be the same as that of the documents they represent, that if the documents are classified, the cards should be in a dictionary order of subjects; that the two sequences, in short, should be complementary. But, apart from the great difficulty of making a satisfactory alphabetical list of subject headings for modern research subjects, this assumes that the reader uses the catalogue as a *supplement* to the shelves, which is not true; he uses it as an *alternative*, that is, the cards stand in the place of the documents as long as he is consulting the catalogue, because the cards form a complete record of the stock, whereas many of the documents may be away on loan. The arrangement of the cards should therefore be the same as that of the documents they represent: if a classified sequence is helpful for them, as is commonly agreed, it will be helpful for the cards also.

There is this much truth in the assumption, however: a classified sequence, whether of cards or documents, is usually arranged in the order of the code, or notation, but readers think in words. There must therefore be a link provided between the reader's words and the filing numbers, which means, as I have already remarked, that the alphabetical author and subject indexes are essential parts of a classified catalogue.

Before discussing indexes, however, I may mention that in certain circumstances the classified file can be dispensed with, if the need for economy demands some sacrifice. This is when the sequence of documents is always complete, that is, when a dummy is inserted if an original document is removed from the sequence. If this course is adopted, some form of reference should also be put with the documents in place of what would have been analytical entries in the classified file—references to relevant parts of other documents shelved elsewhere in the sequence because they deal mainly with another subject. When the reader consults the index, he finds his class number, and goes straight to the documents, knowing that references to everything the library has will be in the one place. It is unlikely that such a procedure would ever be used with books, but for pamphlets, patents, correspondence files and similar documents it does offer a possible economy, and it is already common practice to insert a dummy card in the sequence when a document of this type is borrowed. The dummy should show not merely the identifying number of the document it replaces, but enough of its subject to let the searcher know whether or not it would be useful to him.

So much has been written about making an author catalogue or index that it is hardly necessary to add any more than a conventional warning about the frequent difficulty of finding the true author of certain documents from research organizations—particularly the glorified laboratory reports dealt with in Chapter IX. In the U.S.A., moreover, the tendency seems to be for more and more scientists to work either on secret programmes directly or indirectly for the Government, or in the laboratories of one organization doing work sponsored by some other organization. This may in time lead to some drastic additions and amendments to our codes of cataloguing rules, but it is quite clear that—as in the whole of scientific literature—this is not going to the source of the trouble, which is the chaotic state of publishing.

I should be reluctant to persuade anyone to accept my views on cataloguing this kind of material, since they are in direct contradiction to long-accepted practice. I do not think author entries are worth the time and trouble. Readers in the information library want information for its own sake, not because it has been written by any particular author, and even if they do ask for a report by a name, it is unlikely to be the "correct" one—if indeed anyone can decide what the correct one is. However, it is traditionally demanded that every separate publication shall be catalogued under its author's name, and no doubt most libraries accept this.

When we come to indexes of periodical articles, however, I feel on stronger ground, especially in technology. I consider that it is a waste of time for a library to make its own author index for articles from periodicals, except where the author is very well known to the organization to which the library belongs. An immense amount of labour goes into the construction of such an index, and it is hardly ever the only clue given in a particular request. The periodicals and abstracting journals publish their own indexes—many of them have an author index in each issue—and the gain in convenience is so small as to be quite out of proportion to the cost. On the other hand, one should index freely under the names of people and organizations whose work is well known; this pays handsome dividends. But the final arbiter should be, as always: do the readers need this, or not?

Very much less attention has been paid to the indexing of subjects, though in recent years we have seen a number of new methods that are worth studying. One that the inventor claims to retrieve more than a straight subject search is the Citation Index of Eugene Garfield. This is compiled by linking up each paper with the references quoted by the author and those in which it is itself quoted, and Garfield claims that it is bound to be of great value to a searcher because it provides a complete case history, as it were, for each paper. He has shown that the method will on occasion pick up more relevant papers than the index to *Chemical Abstracts*. It is an ingenious proposal, but can hardly be systematic. Even American writers, who have got into the habit of quoting a reference for the most banal commonplaces, often miss important papers, and few research workers can claim to be familiar with many publications in languages other than their own. Once again, one must measure the cost of compilation against the number of times the record would be the *only* way of reaching the objective.

The Co-ordinate Indexing of Mortimer Taube and his associates in Documentation, Inc., is chiefly remarkable for the violence of the controversy it has set off in the U.S.A., so much so that it is difficult to come to an objective judgment. It may be included in a new comparative project to be set up by Aslib at the Royal College of Aeronautics, Cranfield, which aims at testing several methods of information retrieval by use on the same documents. The Co-ordinate Index contains a series of cards, each headed by a Uniterm—a subject word chosen from a special list. Each document indexed is given a number; it is then analyzed by subject into the appropriate Uniterms, and its number entered on each of the cards headed with these Uniterms. Thus when numerous documents have been indexed, each card may be expected to carry several numbers. In use, the subject sought is analyzed into its Uniterms, the appropriate cards selected and compared, and those numbers that appear on each card will refer to relevant documents. Superficially, this seems a good system; but one has only to visualize the task of picking out perhaps two or three common numbers from several groups each containing dozens, or even hundreds! To have to do this for every enquiry would seem, to put it mildly, tiresome, and we await the results from Cranfield with keen anticipation.

The method of indexing that to me shows most promise at

47

present is the "chain procedure", often adopted instinctively by skilful indexers, and first described systematically by Ranganathan. The *British National Bibliography* has been indexed in this way since it began, but to obtain the full benefit the method needs to be worked in conjunction with a faceted classification. It is based on the fact that while a classification system must choose one sequence, and so can display only one set of relationships, readers may approach their material from other aspects, and these must be entered in the alphabetical subject index as efficiently and as economically as possible. In classifying the subject of a document, its component parts, or facets, have to be put into one particular sequence, and the facet that comes first will be the one at which the document is shelved. The criterion for choosing which one comes first is that of helpfulness to the user: at which facet do most users want their documents grouped?

Consider the subject "the preservation of bacon by irradiation with gamma rays". In the class Food Technology, it is the Product that is the principal focus of the users' interests, and the Product is therefore the first facet:

Product	Operation
Meat : Bacon :	Preservation : Irradiation : Gamma rays
F53831 :	393

The point we are now considering is that the reader may be interested in any one of these five aspects, and all of them must therefore be used as an index entry word. It is not, however, necessary to permute the five to produce 120 entries, because all the reader wants is an entry to the right place in the classified sequence; once there, the subject is displayed before him, by guide cards in a card catalogue, by "feature" headings on a printed page (such as the *British National Bibliography*), or by guides and book titles on the shelves. In chain indexing, the method is to reverse the order of facets from that given in the class number, and then index each facet in turn with only those that now follow it:

Gamma rays:Irradiation:Preservation:Bacon	F53831:393
Irradiation:Preservation:Bacon	F53831:39
Preservation:Bacon	F53831:3
Bacon	F53831
Meat	F538

When beginning a new index, it would also of course be necessary to put in index cards for Food Technology, and Technology, but it is obvious that one card covers all future documents; this is true of every card, but the more specific the subject, the more entries likely to be required.

Similarly, with the subject "the lighting of underground roadways in coal mines", the facet analysis is Coal mines:Roadways: Lighting, and the index entries are:

Lighting:Roadways:Mines, coal	BecCbEpd
Roadways :Mines, coal	BecCb
Mines, coal	Bec
Coal mines	Bec

Thus the subject index entries are closely linked with the place chosen in the classification system, and the act of classifying is shown to be one and the same as the act of choosing subject headings.

The notation or coding shown on the right hand side of these examples is the link between the catalogue and the place the document occupies on the shelves of the library, and enables the catalogue to fulfil its function of acting as a guide to location. Until quite recently, discussions on notation took place on a somewhat superficial level, and in fact resolved themselves into entirely subjective arguments over whether a sequence of symbols all of one type ("pure notation") was easier or harder to use than a sequence containing more than one type ("mixed notation"). Both forms have their supporters, but it seems relatively unimportant, provided that two main qualities are present in as a high degree as possible:(1) the symbols should be at once recognizable as conveying a sequence, and (2) they should give as brief a symbol as is compatible with distinctive identification of every facet of a subject. On the occasions when these two requirements conflict, I should go for the first, and achieve recognizability even at the cost of an extra digit or two. Ranganathan has lately gone to extreme lengths in using several types of symbol to achieve maximum brevity, and in using the Colon Classification I have found this to be a cause of difficulty for staff as well as readers.

During recent years, however, discussion has reached a much higher level, with some valuable theoretical work from Vickery, and a striking, not to say brilliant, contribution from Coates, which has been used for the notation of the *British Catalogue of Music*. It is impossible to do justice to Coates' device in a few words, but he appears to have solved one of the major difficulties, that of distinctively marking each facet without either wasting a digit to use as a marker, or losing the possibility of dividing the terms in one facet by those in another without causing confusion with existing subdivisions of the first. In Food Technology, for example, we use the colon to mark division by terms from the Operations facet, and the number F5311 (Milk and special milks) is distinct from F53:11 (Transport of dairy products); but the colon is really a wasted digit as far as division goes. Coates, using the alphabet, allots only part of it to each facet, and allows the later parts of the alphabet to be divided by the earlier directly. To avoid confusion, division within a facet always begins at the letter after the first letter used in the facet.

D	Choral music
DK	Anthems
EZ	Unaccompanied choral works
G	Male voices
GEZ	Unaccompanied male voices.
GEZDK	Anthems for unaccompanied male voices

So far, this has only been published as applied to music, where it works well because it is a simple and well-defined subject. In making a classification for a special subject with several facets, however, difficulties may arise from the need to spread the alphabet over all the facets, which would produce long numbers unrelieved by any breaking-up device. The alternative is to use more than one alphabet (two are used in Music) but this brings with it the need for facet indicators which, like the colon above, are really wasted digits. They have no meaning, but are mere separators. More experiments are needed to bring out the full potentialities of this notation.

Finally, it is necessary to mention another form of indexing that has inspired a mountain of paper, namely, the various systems of coding devised for use with punched cards. The idea of using machinery is very attractive, and without doubt for a small index—a personal index for instance—the edge-punched card offers a high degree of flexibility with a minimum number of cards; it thus suits very well those who (like most of us) dislike card indexes and have an aversion to proliferating entries even when it is the only way to cover all approaches. But it has to be admitted that so far no machine sorting has been strikingly successful; it may be because the machines now available have not been designed to do this particular job, and their makers are more concerned to turn round the job to suit the machine than vice versa.

I am not yet convinced, however, that a machine will ever be better than a classified index for the specific task of locating a document or a piece of information. Consider the operations involved:

> reading the document,
> coding the document,
> typing the card,
> punching the code on the card, and
> checking the card.

The card is now ready to be filed, and it will be evident that little or no work has so far been saved; it is true that there are no subject index cards, but on the other hand there is the punching to be done, and this is not such a speedy operation as might be thought.

For making a search, there are advantages and disadvantages. The only machines worth considering, for economic reasons, will search about 30,000 cards an hour. If the punched cards are filed in random sequence, this saves time in filing, but every card has to be searched for every enquiry. This means that no enquiry, however straightforward, can be satisfied in less than the time taken to search *all* the cards. If this is not good enough, the cards must be grouped, which means time spent in filing, as with the classified index, and so loses the one outstanding advantage of punched cards. On the other hand, the machine once set will do the searching, and the enquirer can do something else while waiting for his cards, since no human attention is necessary. With the classified index, the searcher has to scan the cards himself, but he may—in fact he should in most cases—find the right code numbers quickly and so move on to the actual documents.

When the machine has finished searching, it has produced only a pack of cards. If a bibliography is wanted, this pack of cards can be handed to a typist, though it will almost certainly be necessary to examine the cards (a) to reject any not suitable for the purpose of the bibliography, and (b) to arrange them in a reasonably systematic order. If the documents themselves are wanted, further reference must be made from the card to the document; and for this purpose, either the documents must be arranged in the sequence of the punching code, or the card must carry another symbol to indicate the location of the document. Personally, I consider that, when compiling a bibliography, it is always advisable to consult the documents if possible, even though the card may carry an abstract, because it is always possible that new trains of thought may be set in motion through each author's association of ideas.

Nevertheless, the considerable interest shown in punched card equipment for documentation may in due course lead to machines developed primarily for the task of literature searching. This should be kept in mind in making any new classification system, so that it is not difficult to adapt it for use with sorting machines if suitable ones become available. For the time being, however, with a good classification system and indexes, most enquiries should be satisfied much more quickly than they could be with a machine. It must also be remembered that, unless set up to deal with several enquiries before operations commence (and these must subsequently be disentangled), an enquiry received after sorting has begun will have to wait until it is finished, when the process must be begun all over again.[1]

Part of the Washington International Conference on Scientific Information will be devoted to problems of arrangement and indexing, and it is probably true to say that more research is going on in these fields than on any other aspect of librarianship. The international conference on classification held at Dorking in May 1957 recommended that the Washington Conference should seriously consider the sponsoring of a new general classification system, and this has since been supported by a resolution sent to the Library Association by the Reference and Special Libraries Section. The production of such a new system, based on facet analysis and suitable for depth classification, would make an outstanding contribution towards solving some of the pressing problems facing us in the documentation of research.

FURTHER READING

I have appended a fairly extensive bibliography to my chapter on Classification in the Aslib *Handbook*. Since then, there has been a new edition of Ranganathan's *Prolegomena*, published by the Library Association, 1957, and the Classification Research Group's *Bulletin* has begun to appear. Two general articles are: B. C. Vickery: "Developments in subject indexing", *J. Doc.*, Vol. 11, No. 1, 1955, pp. 1-11, and D. J. Foskett: "Modern

---

[1] Mr A. J. Wells of the *BNB* informs me that the useful life of a frequently-used punched card is very short, because of the rough handling received in the machine.

trends in classification", in *Communications* of the International Congress of Libraries and Documentation Centres, Brussels 1955. Vol. IIB, pp. 96-102.

Perhaps the best contribution that has so far appeared from E. J. Coates is in the *Technical Problems of Reference and Special Libraries*, Library Association, R.S.L. Section, 1958.

A criticism of some of the claims of punched card enthusiasts was made by Vickery in *American Documentation*, Vol. 2, No. 2, 1951, pp. 102-107.

Perhaps the best survey of recent developments is the Proceedings of the Dorking Conference published by Aslib, 1958.

See *J. Doc.*, Vol. 13, No. 3, 1957, pp. 152-155.

CHAPTER FIVE

Dissemination of Information

IF most of the research and original thinking in the information
library field has centred on arrangement and indexing, by far
the greatest emphasis in practice lies on the dissemination of
information. In fact, it may truly be said that this is the characteristic activity of the special library, distinguishing it, more than
any other feature, from university and public libraries. Many—
it may even be most—special libraries have paid little attention to
"correct" or orthodox methods of selection, acquisition, arrangement and indexing; often their records are scarcely adequate even
by the lowest standards, and it has not been unknown for eminent public librarians, in their wisdom, to utter words of scorn on
this account. But in the matter of dissemination, the special
libraries are far ahead; and this, in my view, is true librarianship,
by whatever name it may be called.

Most libraries nowadays adopt some method of keeping their
readers informed about the material coming into their stock. The
days of merely inserting cards in the catalogue and posting up
some of the brighter dust jackets are passing. But just as there are
various levels in enquiry work, so there are various levels of dissemination, and the better the library, the higher the level it will
reach. In the old days, cards were inserted in the catalogue, it was
said, to answer certain enquiries that readers might make, on
authors, subjects, and so forth. The implication, indeed the
assumption, was that the reader came to the library knowing
what he wanted to read, and used the catalogue—and the librarian too for that matter—to find whether what he wanted was in
stock, and if so, where it was located. He was assumed to be
bibliographically prepared and self-contained; his reading

interests were his own business. He did not want to be told what to look for, but where to find what he knew about already.

It is characteristic of the information library, on the other hand, that it serves a group of people who have a recognized dominant interest—which the library shares. In advancing the interests of its readers, it automatically advances its own. And by the division of labour prevailing in such groups, the library staff are made responsible for the bibliographical preparedness of the whole group, no member of which is self-contained, all being dependent in some way on the others. It is an association of experts, each contributing to the best of his ability, and each able to call on the expertize of the others. The province of the library is the literature: hence the well-known thesis of Farradane, that the information scientist is not a librarian but the particular member of a research group who uses the literature on behalf of the others, working in the library and not in the laboratory.

It is clear that one of the basic requirements for a worker of this type is an extensive knowledge of the interests of his colleagues; indeed, the extent of this knowledge absolutely determines the success of his service. This is another reason why it is in the industrial research department—usually a comparatively small and closely-knit unit—that information libraries have reached their peak of performance.

The basis for dissemination must be the examination of every new document received in the library, to decide whether it is related to the work of any other members of the organization. If it is, it should be brought to their attention at once. The regular circulation of periodicals is the most universally adopted method of ensuring that research staff keep up-to-date in their special fields, but, as is expressed in Bradford's well-known Law of Scattering, articles on one subject frequently appear in periodicals dealing mainly with another. Articles on information work, for example, appear in scientific journals. In such cases, it is the duty of the information officer to see that the article, in addition to its normal circulation, also goes to those interested in its special subject. This sounds simple; but it implies a heavy responsibility and a great deal of work if done well, and if done badly or inconsistently merely irritates, because of the uncertainty created in the readers' minds: they do not know whether their service is reliable or not.

The same practice should be adopted for all new separate publications, books, pamphlets, specifications, regulations, and so on, and it is particularly important that documents like these last two, which lay down standards of performance, should be circulated quickly. Many special libraries serve research workers whose advice is often sought by outside organizations, and they must therefore always be informed of the latest developments of this sort. From the information point of view, there is probably not the same urgency about books; but I should always recommend the circulation of new books, even if only so that research staff can get to know about them. Once informed of their existence, they can read them later, at leisure. It is better to circulate a book twice, in fact, than to wait for each man to read it on the first round. This individual service is of the greatest importance in commercial research, where information very often has to be acted on as quickly as possible if trading advantage is to be won.

So much for the distribution of individual documents to individuals: knowledge of interests combined with a sense of urgency are the prime factors. This must be supplemented by the more formal, comprehensive provision of all things to all men, illustrated by regularly-published bulletins of one sort or another. The most frequently found is the straightforward bulletin of recent additions. Nearly all special libraries, and many libraries of other types, issue these lists and circulate them more or less widely among their readers. It goes almost without saying that such lists, unless they are so frequent that they are quite short, should be arranged is systematic order of subjects. In addition to such lists of accessions, most libraries now produce lists of books on particular subjects—selective bibliographies—either to satisfy a particular enquiry or because a subject has assumed a topical interest for the library users.

Another useful bulletin, but one that is found less commonly, is a news bulletin, giving items of current general information, for example about forthcoming meetings and conferences. Some of the societies themselves publish a news bulletin, like *Chemistry and Industry* and *Chemical and Engineering News*, and while many research journals carry only articles, nearly all trade journals contain a good deal of this kind of current information. It is important that research staff (and library staff too) should have the opportunity to go to professional meetings, and this is being encouraged more and more in industry. It follows automatically that the library should play its particular role in this sphere as in others; fortunately it does not require any specialized knowledge to compile a news bulletin, and it can be done by a typist from marked copies of journals and leaflets, unless of course something a little more elaborate is desirable, when it should be written by a senior member of the information staff.

An interesting practice which has been made much simpler by new developments in document copying is that of circulating, or posting on a notice board, copies of the Contents pages of journals as they are received. This can be a formidable undertaking where there is a large number of subscriptions, but no other method brings new work to general notice so quickly. It has become very popular in the U.S.A., and a commercial publication has actually been launched to provide *Contents in Advance*. The accuracy of the title is very much open to speculation, though the compilers claim to work from advance proofs. A few periodicals publishers also give the contents of one of their journals in another: the *Journal of Scientific Instruments* and the *British Journal of Applied Physics* are examples of this mutual service. If the publishing of research work were an organized affair instead of the present chaos, advance lists of contents might well be supplied to subscribers as part of the subscription; it would save a deal of work and would certainly be appreciated.

The Society of Chemical Industry sets a good example here by giving in each issue the titles of papers accepted for future publication.

The great standard form of publication for the special library, of course, is the bulletin of abstracts, of which there must be many hundreds produced for private circulation. On the face of it, this is a terrible waste of time and labour, but when we examine the problem in detail, it becomes evident that the particular circumstances in which each is produced usually justify its existence. An information officer must consider very seriously, before starting such a bulletin, whether or not his trouble can be saved by use of published abstracts. The answer to this question usually depends on two factors: first, whether there is a single publication that meets his needs, or whether he must buy several to get complete coverage; and second, how many copies he needs for his readers to get their abstracts reasonably promptly. Usually the first factor is the deciding one; if the whole, or nearly the whole of an organization's interests are covered by a single journal, it is pointless to duplicate it. This may well be the case in a specialized industry served by a Research Association, or in an industry, like the chemical and electrical engineering industries, which is served by a long-established journal with the requisite wide coverage. Happy indeed is the information officer who can rely on such services: he saves himself many headaches, and probably covers many more periodicals than he could afford to buy.

Another important factor that may decide the issue, even against the first two, is the pattern of the organization. In larger firms particularly, there may be several branches—factories, research sub-stations, administrative units, overseas stations—which require not only to receive but also to keep their file of abstracts. At the present rate of subscription, it would hardly be economical for a specialized firm in the chemical industry to buy many copies of *Chemical Abstracts* for distribution. To produce its own bulletin would be cheaper and would also get the abstracts out more quickly.

Supposing, then, that the information officer has decided to produce his own abstracts, he must consider (1) what type of abstract to use, (2) whether to appoint an abstractor or use the research staff, and (3) what method of reproduction to use.

Of the two established types of abstract, the indicative and the informative, the latter is always to be preferred if it can be afforded. Even if it appears to be too expensive, the cost of supplying the original articles to readers must be taken into account: this is likely to be far higher when the abstracts are only indicative. It is very difficult indeed to write good indicative abstracts, furthermore, and some of those published provide good illustrations of completely uninformative strings of clichés, often doing no more than paraphrase a title.

An informative abstract, that is, an abstract that actually contains the gist of the information in an article, meets much more satisfactorily both of the requirements of an abstracting journal. It keeps the reader generally up-to-date with the subject, and it helps much more in a retrospective search. With indicative abstracts, which more or less only name the subject of an article, one nearly always needs to go back to the original; informative abstracts, on the other hand, often contain the particular piece of information that the enquirer wants. This consideration carries particular weight when the abstracts are sent to readers who are not within easy reach of a good library. It is well worth while spending more money making good abstracts for the sake of even only one or two people whose access to the literature is severely limited—in foreign countries, for example. The abstracts of the Commonwealth Agricultural Bureaux are outstandingly good publications built up with the particular needs of isolated research workers in mind.

During the early years of information services, it was customary for the abstracting to be shared out among the research staff, not merely because of lack of information assistants, but more because it seemed the natural course to adopt. They would be reading the journals anyway, and their specialized knowledge would give extra value to the abstracts they wrote. The trend now is for abstracts to be written by the information staff, and more attention is being paid to training in abstracting technique; lectures are being given in some of the Schools of Librarianship. On the whole, I think a better bulletin can be produced by skilled abstractors. Despite the advantages of using research staff, they seem to have generally regarded the work as something outside the scope of their proper duties, and to have accorded it rather less than its rightful share of their time. Far from ensuring that those abstracting read their journals more quickly than they might otherwise have done, the responsibility often resulted in journals being put on one side, to await a period of greater leisure—which probably rarely materialized. The professional abstractor is more reliable in time, more consistent in style, and with proper training soon acquires familiarity with the subjects he writes about, even though he may not have known much about them at the outset. This is not to underestimate the value of subject knowledge; but, like librarians and information officers, the abstractor needs a wide range rather than a great depth of knowledge, it being unlikely that he will have both.

Even more useful than bulletins of abstracts are surveys of the literature on specific topics. The practice of making a literature search before beginning a piece of research is now well-established, and no doubt most research workers prefer to do their own searching. As far as their own work is concerned, they are the ones with the prepared minds. No rules or principles can be laid down for deciding who should take this responsibility; so much depends on the circumstances and on the attitude of the research man who will ultimately do the project. The least a librarian can do, however, is to make a thorough search for items of potential interest, and to ensure that the research man knows how to set about making his own search. At the other end of the scale, there are many who will gladly be rid of the task, and are content to trust the information staff to produce a summary of the state of the art.

Coming more clearly within the scope of the library is the survey produced, not as a preliminary to a research programme, but as a general statement on a subject for wide distribution to the other departments. This amounts to assembling as much information as possible, from all sources (including human ones), and writing it as a story in an interesting style; very often such surveys are principally for the benefit of non-specialists, and great care needs to be taken to produce something that will make easy reading and be readily understood.

The communication of knowledge is a subject which has burst upon the scene with almost explosive force, and has brought into being an enormous literature in a very short time. Since it is of interest to every specialist, contributions have come from philosophers, philologists, logicians, mathematicians, physicists, biologists, electrical engineers; and in the midst of the mountains of paper, those who deplore the present-day over-specialization may derive some small ray of hope from the spectacle of a professor of linguistics contributing, in the *Journal of the Acoustical Society of America*, to the same symposium as a telephone engineer.

It would be beyond my scope and competence to discuss this subject in the detail it deserves, but one important aspect of communication must not be overlooked when considering the production of information bulletins. Indiscriminate circulation without regard to the nature of various groups of readers can do a good deal of harm, particularly with scientific material in an industrial firm. While the practising scientist can face a bulletin of abstracts because he is accustomed to using such things, they have little or no appeal for the average factory man, who might benefit equally from the information they contain. Similarly, it is worse than useless to present a 50-page bibliography on metal-working to an accountant wishing to improve his general knowledge of production methods. He would not only refuse to look at it; he would also regard it as a sign that the library was ridiculously out-of-touch with its readers' needs.

We must therefore study the techniques of presenting specialized information to readers of different intellectual levels. The
same material can be made readily acceptable to dissimilar groups
if presented to each in a manner suitable to its educational background. For some years, the Research Department Library of the
Metal Box Company has been distributing two bulletins, an
Information Letter and a Survey of Literature. The first contains
summaries of articles, patents and pamphlets, and book reviews,
and is written in an informal, critical style, relating their contents
to the work of the Company where possible. This is directed to
factories, sales, administrative and engineering departments, and
has been notably successful in communicating information on
new technical and scientific developments to this wide general
audience. The Survey of Literature contains the usual type of
informative abstract, and is directed particularly to the scientific
staff. The difference between the two may perhaps be expressed
by saying that an abstract speaks with the voice of the original
author, but the Information Letter speaks with its own voice and
comments on what the authors have written. Two of the
Research Associations have recently begun to produce similar
Information Letters, also aimed particularly at the staffs of their
members' factories.

A direct result of issuing all these bulletins is that the librarian
and information officer has to consider carefully what method he
will use to reproduce them. Until quite recently, the almost universal practice was to type on a wax stencil, and this remains the
most favoured method. Where a higher standard is required, as
when the document is sold, ordinary letterpress printing has been
the rule; many Research Associations print their news and
abstracts journals. Most information services, however, do not
need enough copies to make letterpress printing economical, and
so such developments as office offset lithographic presses are of
great interest. Where very short runs are usual, a saving over
stencil duplication can probably be made through the cheapest
paper plates, even though running off takes longer because the

63

rollers have to be cleaned after each page. Long runs requiring more expensive paper and ultimately metal plates would not be so cheap as stencil duplication, but the resulting appearance of the work warrants the extra cost. Used in conjunction with a variable-face typewriter which can justify the lines and so produce an even right-hand margin, these presses make formidable competitors with commercial printing, to the extent that great controversy rages over them in the printing and office management journals. This field of activity promises other developments of similar interest, and if librarians take the opportunity, they might well bring about the design of new equipment tailored to their needs, and not, as usually happens, find themselves obliged to take whatever a manufacturer likes to offer in the way of machinery originally intended to do something else. Meanwhile, a subscription to a lively and well-informed journal such as *Office Magazine* brings in a flow of useful information and practical hints; so, for those fortunate enough to receive it, does the Treasury *O & M Bulletin*.

More and more heads of information services are assuming responsibilities for editorial work, not only for their own publications, but also for other documents issued by their department, especially papers submitted for publication by members of the research staff. I would exclude publicity and advertising material, and house journals, from this control, because both of these are highly-skilled jobs calling for specialized staff, and although no doubt purveying information, such documents do not, in my opinion, come within the scope of an information service—on the production end. Signs are not lacking that there are those who would bring all these under an information officer; in fact it becomes more and more difficult to define his scope if we use this denomination literally.

However, since bulletins are definitely part of an information service, the head of it must know enough of editorial technique to produce them efficiently; and since it does not form a recognized part of the duty of any other member of the research group, it seems logical that the editorial work of the group should fall to the information officer. He has the function of distributing within his group information received from outside, so he can well arrange also the distribution to the outside world of information produced by his group. He may need to exercise considerable tact in assuming this responsibility, because research workers are apt to think themselves capable of preparing their own papers for publication.

The first, and probably one of the most difficult parts of such editing is assembling material to meet a publication date. It is notoriously difficult in a scientific department, because many scientists do not like writing and so do not write easily; sometimes they have to be very earnestly persuaded to write at all. As I have said, I believe this to be one of the reasons for the growing use of professional abstractors. With the library's own publications this difficulty may not arise, as most of the work may be done by information staff; but it is highly desirable just the same to use contributions by research staff if possible, especially in pamphlets series, for which this is in fact the most likely source of material. It means that a specialist expert writes on his own subject, in the first place, and it also gives the research staff a sense of participating in a library activity; as a corollary, it demonstrates that the library can on occasion be the means of presenting the group's work to the public. Considerations such as this exercise a certain influence in persuading research workers to offer their contributions and to produce them in reasonable time. In some circumstances, it may of course be necessary to obtain a "security" clearance for the material to be published, and this should be done before the paper is actually written if it does not already exist as a research report.

When the paper has been written, it should be checked for grammar and style. This again requires some tactful dealing with the author, but most authors appreciate that sympathetic criticism is usually helpful and will realize, especially if they are scientists, the importance of presenting their work in as good a style as possible. This often has to be pointed out to them at first; we are constantly being told nowadays that scientists are not interested in presentation, but they are certainly interested in having their papers read, and can soon be brought to see that the better the style, the easier the reading. As the editors of the *Biochemical Journal* remark, however, "easy reading's curst hard writing", and if a librarian or information officer can make suggestions that lighten the task, no sensible scientist will reject them.

The arrangement of the material may occasionally present problems. Arrangement within a single paper naturally comes within the province of the author, who may nevertheless welcome constructive criticism; arrangement of several items in the same publication should be done by the editor. Very often the most suitable arrangement suggests itself, but the editor should always make a conscious decision on the principle on which he proposes to work. This certainly improves the final form of the publication, and also makes it easier for him to defend his arrangement if necessary. For such composite publications, and indeed for all separate publications, he must also decide on format. This is largely a matter of taste, but one point deserves mention because of the suffering—often unnecessary—that it has caused librarians. If possible, the editor of any publications likely to form a series should envisage the future contents, so that he can choose a format that he will not need to change. We have all experienced the changes of size that many periodicals were forced into by the war; that was scarcely avoidable, perhaps. Far more infuriating are the changes of format in, say, pamphlets series, that the editor could have avoided by using a little foresight.

Perhaps the most important services that a librarian can render in an editorial capacity are the checking of references and their citation in an approved style. This matter has received a great deal of attention in science, but not so much in technology; in Literature itself, of course, references are often likely to be to works readily available in many editions. "Almost every librarian and research worker", says Cyril Barnard, "must have suffered from the inconvenience and waste of time caused by imperfect and incorrect references to literature". It seems obvious that references should be made accurately, so that readers of the paper may be able to follow them up without difficulty, but is unfortunately true that even now authors are excessively careless about their manner of citing references, and all too often the details given are inadequate. For example, a reference such as "*Food Engineering*, Vol. 24, 1952, p. 75" forgets that each issue has its own pagination, and that the unlucky searcher will have to begin with issue No. 1 of volume 24, and examine every issue until he finds the right page 75. Similarly, an apparently complete reference such as "*Archives of Industrial Hygiene*, 1952, No. 2, p. 146", is in fact still misleading because there were two volumes of the journal in 1952, and therefore both the February and the August issues were numbered 2. A very complete and valuable survey of this problem was made by Barnard, and British Standard Specification 1629 made a not very well-received attempt to formulate a standard that would be satisfactory without being too cumbersome. It is essential that bibliographies attached to research publications should adopt one or other of the recognized systems, described by Barnard, and follow it consistently.

For the library's own publications, the librarian should decide all these questions of style, arrangement, format and citation, and preferably write a small manual describing his "style of the house". If he can persuade his authors to adopt his rules themselves when they write their papers, he will naturally save himself a deal of work, but this is not always possible; a series of research reports, for example, may have a format not suitable for a printed work, so that a certain amount of editing has to be done if a report is published. Similarly, the librarian can perform a very useful service for his colleagues by collecting as much information as possible on the house style of various journals, so that when they propose to submit papers for publication, they can create a favourable impression on the editor of the journal they choose, by adopting his style in their manuscript.

One of the tasks which arise out of publication and which no one really enjoys is reading and correcting proofs. Consequently a librarian will experience no difficulty whatever in persuading research staff to let him relieve them of this particular job. He should nevertheless ask the author to read the paper through, not necessarily to look for misprints, but to see that no textual errors have crept in that would not be evident to a non-specialist. Ideally, proof correction should be a major operation done by two people, one reading aloud the proof and the other checking the manuscript, but this is not always practicable. A reader working alone should look through his proof twice, once to examine each word individually for misprints, and again to read the text for a final overall check.

While the chief value of information service publications undoubtedly lies in their dissemination of new knowledge, both inside and outside the organization, they also perform another by no means negligible function in helping the library to obtain documents by exchange. In the end, the high prices now being charged by some, especially American and German, journals, may well defeat their own object, as they are encouraging more and more libraries to try to produce their own literature to use in exchange. It must be well known by now that this is a very easy way of obtaining publications from Communist countries, which are unable to buy much foreign material through shortage of currency, but which seem generally to make both national and special material available to their libraries for this purpose. No information library ought to overlook the *Unesco Bulletin for Libraries*, which always carries notices of material offered and wanted by libraries all over the world, and it is often worth sending a specimen copy of one's bulletins to an organization known to be working in one's own fields, with an invitation to enter into an exchange agreement. This seems an elementary point, but

I mention it again here, because although libraries have long benefited from such arrangements, there is still plenty of scope for extending the practice, and currency difficulties look like being prolonged for some time yet.

The other main reason for exchanging, from the point of view of economics, is of course that extra copies of one's own publications are cheaper than the works one receives. Naturally, therefore, the library issuing its own series can effect quite considerable savings as well as obtaining material that might otherwise be difficult or even impossible to get. Now I should point out here that mere annual reports or bulletins of accessions will *not*, as a rule, be accepted in exchange for journals carrying original work! Nevertheless, even if a library cannot produce an acceptable series of abstracts, pamphlets or similar works, it may yet be able to achieve something with reprints of articles by the research staff, which can usually be obtained at a reasonably low cost from the journals publishing them. Some firms overprint a series note on such reprints, while some enclose them in covers bearing the firm's name and the article's title. The possibility of using reprints in this way stresses once again the importance of the librarian's acting as controller of such series of publications.

While one's natural instincts are to eliminate as many records as possible, clearly the distribution lists for library publications must be maintained extremely carefully. Few things arouse more cynicism than to continue mailing bulletins to people who have moved, or retired, or otherwise ceased to be interested. Some libraries now follow the practice of publicity agencies, and periodically ask their readers to check their addresses as used on the label; within an organization, however, retirements, resignations and postings are often circulated in notices, and it is thus necessary for the library to be on the mailing list for these, and for it to check the contents against its own lists. Not only should departures be noted, and those departed struck off the list; it is also a good idea to write at once to the new arrivals and replacements, offering to include them. If a bulletin is useful to one occupant of a post, the chances are that it will also be useful to his successor, and such an action convincingly demonstrates the library's alertness.

There is a minor but quite important detail to be noted in connection with publications having a restricted circulation, such as those that begin life as "Confidential to members". It often happens that in due course they are removed from the "Confidential" category, and then the information in them can be disseminated more widely. A register of recipients should be kept in order that they may be notified of such changes of category. A good method is that used by the British Non-Ferrous Metals Research Association, which attaches to the document one part of a two-part label, the two parts being divided by a row of perforations. The non-attached part carries the "Confidential" legend, and when the document is removed from that category, it is a simple matter to tear off the "Confidential" part of the label and so remove the restriction on the document's circulation.

In my view, libraries should engage in as much of the work of disseminating information as they can, as I think it is the characteristic form of reference service in its most advanced state of development. It has not been possible here to do more than glance at some of the many types of bulletins, of which there are first-class examples, produced by libraries to save the time and labour of research workers. The rapid growth of the movement for dissemination by libraries, and the fact that it is usually welcomed and encouraged by research staff, show that library publications fill a definite social role, largely in scientific research at present, but promising to play a growing part in other fields. And these publications, it should not be forgotten, are even more than a valuable service to research workers; for the librarians who produce them, they form an invaluable means of increasing both their subject knowledge and their mastery of the literature. This leads, in its turn, to a greater competence and an even higher level of service.

Nor does the absence of evaluation, on the level that the research worker himself could give, detract from the value of library bulletins. In certain circumstances, where evaluation is necessary—in bulletins for factories, for example—advice can, and should be obtained from appropriate experts; otherwise, the old fear and distrust felt by the experts for evaluation performed by information workers may well be aroused again, to undermine the confidence built up by efficient performance of our own work without attempting to do everyone else's as well.

FURTHER READING

An important survey of abstracting services was made at the Unesco Conference in 1949: *International Confe ence on Science Abstracting—Final Report.*

The instructions given by editors to their abstractors might also be usefully consulted.

The best small book on style is:

R. O. Kapp: *Presentation of technical information*, Constable, **1948**. See also:

Trelease, S. F.: *The Scientific paper*, Bailliere, 2nd edn,, 1952.

B. C. Vickery: The presentation of information, in the 1955 RSL Conference Proceedings.

C. C. Barnard: Bibliographical citation. *Librarian*, Vol. 39, 1950, pp. 105-110, 171-175, and 125-129 (sic).

A good example of a "style of the house" book has been published by John Wiley, *Authors' guide to preparing manuscripts and handling proof*, 1950.

Two British Standards are also relevant:

B.S. 1219:1945 Printers' and authors' proof corrections, and

B.S. 1629:1950 Bibliographical references.

CHAPTER SIX

Reference Service

DISSEMINATING information that will keep its readers well-informed and up-to-date in their own and related subjects forms one aspect of information service; the second, of equal importance, is the provision of answers to specific enquiries, and this may take several forms according to the nature of the question actually asked. I do not propose to discuss here such essential tools as guides to reference works, encyclopedias, dictionaries, bibliographies; this ground has already been worked over in some detail. All that needs saying here, perhaps, is that one great service that librarians and information officers might render to scholarship is the compilation of extensive bibliographies and guides to the literature of special subjects. The excellent short list given in the Aslib *Handbook* shows up the incompleteness of our coverage, and a few of the works quoted there are indeed written by librarians. But while all agree on the urgent need for similar works in other fields, very few come forward offering to undertake them.

In reference service, the basic qualification is probably experience, through which a librarian acquires the flair that directs him along the paths most likely to lead to the information he wants. There is no substitute for this, and even the most enthusiastic beginner should, if possible, learn the business under the direct guidance of an experienced colleague. The old "apprentice" system continues to work well in industry, and has appeared even in the higher echelons of management in the shape of the "personal assistant". In this way, the important principle of "learning by doing" can be observed, and although it appears time-consuming at first sight, the training gained thereby soon pays dividends. Furthermore, this system provides an initial spell for observation of the qualities of new assistants, enabling the librarian to separate out those whose bent is not for reference work, and to avoid the dangerous practice of letting loose an inexperienced *and* unsuitable assistant on the unfortunate reader— a harrowing experience that can easily destroy for ever a reader's confidence in the library. The importance of a good manner, in fact, can scarcely be over-emphasized for the special library; one need only visualize the impact of a bad manner on, say, the director of research.

Among older librarians it was often said, and it is still said to-day by librarians of the famous "bookman" variety, that flair and manner are the only qualities needed by the true reference librarian. In public libraries, though fortunately nowhere else, this has resulted in the widespread view that reference librarians do not make good administrators; consequently, few chief librarians have much experience of reference service, and few reference librarians have become chiefs. This is one of the more disastrous trends in British public librarianship. In university and special libraries, knowledge of the literature has necessarily gone hand-in-hand with both reference service and administration; the view of a reference librarian as a special class of being scarcely exists. Flair, on its own, does not distinctively characterize anyone.

Nor, in fact, does it suffice for good reference service. It may be that libraries exist where the level of service is so low that all the enquiries received in it are satisfied at once from the stock. The majority, however, certainly receive enquiries that need some research work ending in a communication to the reader at a later date, and this requires a mode of procedure, or routine. C. W. Hanson argues that the bibliographical apparatus varies so much from one subject to another that any system of searching applicable to many "must be so general as to be nearly useless as a practical guide". This may be true; but its corollary is that a librarian who moves from a library specializing in one field to one specializing in another must find his previous experience valueless, and I cannot bring myself to believe that. In another book, *Assistance to Readers in Lending Libraries*, I set out to describe a procedure that had achieved a reasonable degree of success in a public library. I have since found that much the same procedure serves in both a specialized technical library and in a university library, and I believe that the lack of such a routine has been responsible for making reference service "the outstanding failure of British librarianship". Hanson himself, in fact, goes on to give some admirable advice on "finding the answer", and no doubt most special librarians and information officers have evolved for themselves a method of work that they have found will bring them the answers in the most efficient way.

To those who will accuse me of introducing the dreaded bogey of standardization into an essentially intellectual process, I reply that, to me at least, this is one of those many occasions when some standardization means, not tyranny, but freedom from uncertainty and chaos. How many of us have put a question to a reference librarian (or an information officer), and witnessed the humiliating spectacle of a professional colleague floundering about his catalogues and reference books because, not knowing our subject, and having no routine to guide him, he cannot dredge up from the depths of his ignorance the smallest idea of where to begin? I certainly do not advocate attempting to bluff the reader by briskness of manner; by all means admit ignorance of the subject—even an information officer is rarely expected to be omniscient. But it is essential that he should give the impression of knowing how to go about his job. What would Leonardo have replied, one wonders, to anyone who advised him to forget his meticulous, mathematical technique, and rely exclusively on flair? Real flair consists of knowing through experience when to depart from routine, but the routine must exist first.

This does not mean to say that every librarian will behave in a precisely similar manner. There are intricate rules in English grammar, but Fielding does not write in the same style as Dickens. The truth is that we have not yet arrived at the basic principles of reference service, though many librarians and scientists have written about the procedures they use themselves. I believe that further work and thought on the matter is justified, because I have found, even now, among librarians as well as among research workers, a need for some brief practical guidance on how to carry out a survey of the literature.

First, however, it must be remembered that there are two views on the value of a literature search. Not everyone subscribes to the opinion that, because a library search is cheaper than a full-scale research investigation, the former should as a rule come first. Many eminent scientists, among them W. I. B. Beveridge in his very fine book on *The Art of Scientific Investigation*, believe that excessive reading colours the mind and may divert the researcher from the path suggested by his own inspiration. In universities, where training research workers in the techniques of research forms an important part of the programme, this may doubtless be true; but most of the situations in which information services operate do not exist to train people to do research, but to benefit from the results of their research. We can appreciate, therefore, that literature searching may play a valuable role in hastening the arrival of these benefits, but we should nevertheless bear in mind the prevalence of the opposite view.

The first step is to find out what the reader wants, as exactly as possible. Superficially, this might seem easy; in practice it rarely happens that an enquirer can state his needs with precision. Nor should this surprise us. When a research worker begins to make a search, he has become aware of a gap in his knowledge that he wants to fill, but he cannot know the extent of his ignorance. When he formulates the questions he asks, it is more likely to be in terms of what he knows than of what he does not know. Here lies, indeed, the great value of systematic arrangement in libraries: if the answer has been written about, the classification system should ensure that the documents containing it are placed in close relation to those describing the surrounding areas of knowledge—which are usually those in terms of which the enquirer states his question. The librarian is thus guided from the known to the unknown by his professional techniques and his own skill in using them. Of course, knowing the background of the enquiry gives enormous help, and this is easily possible in the special library because part of the duty of the information staff is to know the interests of their research colleagues. It is only to be expected that, with such an advantage, special libraries should have been able to carry reference service up to its highest level in the literature survey.

Generally speaking, we can identify three main lines of approach in reference service:

(1) the author/title approach, in which the reader names a document or group of documents: "Do you have the *Journal of Experimental Psychology*?"

(2) the factual approach, in which the reader names a specific fact: "What is the specific heat of mercury?"

(3) the subject approach, in which the reader names, as nearly as he can, the subject of his interest: "Have you anything on the teaching of number in primary schools?"

The first of these presents no difficulty and can be answered by referring to the library's own catalogue and to appropriate bibliographies. The second requires that knowledge of sources gained by study, training and experience, and therefore underlines the importance of these. Even in the most specialist of libraries, factual enquiries may range over the entire field of knowledge because of the possibility of an infinity of relationships among actual phenomena. Excellent advice has been given by a number of experts on how to deal with such enquiries; perhaps the best and the best known appear in A. D. Roberts' *Introduction to Reference Books* and in C. W. Hanson's chapter in the Aslib *Handbook*.

The third category of request has become the most important and the most frequently received, at least in information libraries. Because of the great expansion of research, and the growing specialization of knowledge, it is also the most difficult. The answer generally takes the form of a bibliography or a literature survey. Either may be passed to the reader on paper or by word of mouth, and either may comprise one item or many.

The factual and the subject approaches merge at their boundaries, and a literature search may be necessary for each. The difference is that when the answer to the first is found, the search ends, whereas a subject search with the object of compiling a bibliography or survey can never truly be said to have ended. *Pace* Hanson, there is no such thing as a *complete* bibliography. This melancholy reflection arises from the vast amount of material published and the haphazard methods of recording it; and also from experience.

Before consulting any source, the searcher must be sure that he has placed the subject of the enquiry in its correct part of the field of knowledge, and he does this by classifying it. In other words, he must analyse the subject into its various facets, which not only clarifies it in his own mind, but also provides him with the key words under which he will have to look when he comes to indexes and catalogues. He soon finds that each facet may appear in other complex subjects in relation with yet other facets, and helpful information may be found in all these places.

Consider the example already given: "the teaching of number in primary schools", which has three facets, teaching, number, primary schools. Each of these is a sub-division of a larger class: education methods, arithmetic, schools. Each may appear in other contexts, without relation to the other two: for example, "the psychology of teaching methods", "the theory of number", "basic curriculum in primary schools". Documents dealing with any of these three may be of use to the enquirer. It is not enough, therefore, simply to consult references dealing with the specific subject in its entirety: each of its facets may lead to other helpful material.

As Hanson points out, the best way of working is from the general to the particular, so that it is usually best to begin with the latest general works on the subject or on the "main class" that contains it, especially if there happens to be a good work of reference ("Manual", "Encyclopedia", "Dictionary", etc.). The facet analysis of the subject acts as a guide to the places in indexes and tables of contents that are likely to produce the information required. It is usually at this stage that flair takes the biggest part, in suggesting ways of shortening the search by going directly to a more specialized or not so obvious source in which it may be easier to locate more, and more detailed, information.

With the present rate and cost of publication, the information may not yet have appeared in book form, and the next source is the periodical article or pamphlet. Scientists are more fortunate than some other research workers in that most of their material of this kind is picked up by the abstracting services in due course, but the obvious benefits of this are being perceived by the others, and indexes and abstracts are becoming increasingly familiar in the social sciences and even in the humanities. It will sometimes happen, with a factual enquiry, that an abstract contains all the information required; for example, a search for the ash content of tamarind fruit can be answered at once by reference to the subject index to *Chemical Abstracts*, which leads to the abstract of an article containing analytical data for tamarind, published in *Chronica Naturae* in 1948. Because so many enquiries of this type are received, abstracts obviously make much better library tools than mere indexes. Often, however, it will be necessary to consult the original article, and this should certainly be done when there is any doubt as to whether or not the abstract will answer the enquiry completely. Abstracts cannot possibly even indicate the whole contents of their originals, and the same article may be abstracted in entirely different ways for periodicals dealing with different aspects of the same subject.

If the search of indexes and abstracting journals fails to produce the desired result, the next step must be to search the indexes to the individual journals themselves, choosing of course the most likely ones. As will be readily appreciated, this is somewhat time-consuming, but it is forced on the searcher in those fields not well served by abstracts, and even in those that are, there is always the chance that useful information may have been overlooked by an abstractor or may be contained in material that does not usually find its way into abstracting journals. Some trade and technical journals, for example, have a section of useful hints, answers to enquiries, recipes and similar information, much of which is never abstracted but is often indexed by the journal's own index.

Before embarking on such a lengthy task, however, it may be preferable to consult some other organization. There are many directories of such sources, well known to librarians, and the telephone directory will often give a useful lead under a catchword included in the name of an organization. The Tin Research Institute, for example, has a great deal of information about making tin cans, and like many similar organizations is very willing to lend and even give it. The editorial departments of some of the specialized journals are a valuable source of information, and some of them maintain Information and Advice Bureaux which welcome enquiries and publish the answers in the journal. One should not, generally speaking, try an outside source before making a reasonably thorough investigation of one's own material, but no librarian or research worker would refuse to answer an enquiry if he can, or give a lead to a likely source. If therefore it seems likely that an organization could be expected to provide an immediate answer to an enquiry without much trouble, the sensible step is to contact that organization early on. On the other hand, it is wrong to expect another organization to accept an enquiry if it means that its staff will have to carry out searching that the enquirer is able to do himself.

If the enquiry is of a wide scope, the general indexes and bibliographies may be of use. Many countries publish national bibliographies, and while these cannot be expected to take the place of abstracting journals (nor do they pretend to), they form very useful complements, and may on occasion include items that have been omitted from the abstracting journals, some of which do not review books at all. The Library Association's *Subject Index to Periodicals* and the many specialized indexes of the H. W. Wilson Company may be worth searching; and the *British National Bibliography* increases its value to the information library every year by the number of specialist monographs that it includes.

All these sources have to be consulted when the object of the search is to make a survey or bibliography, but as there is no single question to be answered, there is really no point at which the search can be said to have ended. Indeed, it is a depressing feature of these surveys that new and often vitally important items continue to appear after the work has gone to press or reached its final form. There is no solution, however; even a public announcement that the work is approaching finality will not halt the progress of knowledge, and the compiler must therefore accept the inevitable and hope to make his work as nearly complete as conscientious and systematic labour can.

One piece of advice that seems elementary is that one should find out whether a bibliography exists already; so many subjects have been covered that this is not unlikely. But it is also likely that one will have to add to it—to fill in gaps or bring it up-to-date—and, apart from general sources such as the *World Bibliography of Bibliographies*, the steps that have to be taken in order to find the bibliography are the same as those taken to start the search if no bibliography exists.

In this type of search, system and method are even more important than in the search for factual answers. It is possible that such an answer may be published more than once, and so be reachable by more than one route; this does not matter, since the search ends as soon as the answer is found. But while many articles may be abstracted and indexed more than once, there remains a large number that are not, and, in addition, a systematic approach should mean that the searcher need not have to go to the same source twice.

As with the factual enquiry, the first step is to analyse the subject into its facets as precisely as possible, before beginning the search, and use these facets as key words for entering indexes. An early step should be to consult the catalogue of a specialist library, if there is one, especially if it compiles its own subject index to the periodicals it receives. Most librarians are pleased to make their resources available for research of this kind, and they know the main sources of information in their field. Even assuming that the bibliographer can begin in his own library, he should nevertheless visit others, to ensure that he does not overlook important material which may not have been discovered through abstracts and indexes, but which is almost certain to exist. The main advantage of taking this step early in the search is that the material is already arranged in an order convenient for consultation. It is always highly desirable to discover references in the place where the documents that they refer to are located, since it saves the bibliographer (and several other people) the necessity of going through the routine of inter-library loan. This saving is particularly appreciated where numerous references are involved.

The next step is to consult the indexes of books and abstracting and indexing journals under each facet of the subject. A note is made of each reference as it is found, and after two or three indexes have been consulted, a few journals will have emerged as being the most likely sources. In making a survey, it is always desirable to have a look at the original articles if possible, for several reasons. It is essential to confirm that the article really is important to the survey, and to supplement where necessary the information contained in the abstract. Equally essential is the actual checking of the details of the reference; errors can occur, and the reputation of any bibliography is seriously damaged if a reference that has simply been copied turns out to be wrong. In addition, the articles themselves frequently contain bibliographies with references to other articles not found previously. Reference to the most-often found journals should not, however, be confined to articles found in this way. Although a somewhat heavy task, it is a good idea to look through the entire file of the journal, because this often brings to light relevant information contained in other articles, not dealing primarily with the topic being surveyed, which for that reason have not been indexed by the abstracting journals under the headings consulted. This is also a good way of discovering useful information from advertisements, which as far as I know are never abstracted.

A detailed search of this type will only be economically feasible for those journals that are indicated as major sources. On the other hand, Bradford's Law shows that articles on a given subject are likely to be widely scattered, and the important thing is never to overlook any abstracting or indexing journal that may refer to relevant material, including general sources such as national bibliographies.

I have already mentioned specialist libraries as valuable sources; equally important are specialist individuals. All librarians, I am sure, use the telephone constantly in answering enquiries, and yet some information officers seem to take it for granted that one feature of their work that distinguishes them from librarians is that they make use of personal contacts. This is a favourite argument of the D.S.I.R. Intelligence Division, who do not claim to know all about every subject, but to know where to find the appropriate specialist, as well as the appropriate literature. One of the most useful indexes that an information library can maintain is a directory of such specialists who are willing to help answer enquiries, and librarians and information officers do an enormous amount to help each other. This is one reason why professional activity is so valuable; at meetings and in committees one meets colleagues from libraries specializing in all fields, and I myself have received invaluable help from friends all over the world. So useful is this network of contacts that it is quite well known outside the profession; more than once have satisfied readers commented that there seems to be a mutual aid society among librarians. Fortunately, the information officers who like to distinguish themselves by this characteristic are usually willing to give information to librarians, even though by the very act of doing so they would appear to be eliminating the distinction.

As each source is consulted, a summary giving the important points should be made, in a form of record that is flexible. The survey is likely to have a number of sub-divisions, and it will be helpful if during the search the material is collected in such a way that the final arrangement becomes simple. For example, to use a notebook starting at the front and working through gives no flexibility whatever and provides no means for putting together articles on the same aspect or sub-division of the subject. Two other forms give much greater flexibility: loose-leaf notebooks, and individual cards or sheafs.

It is frequently stated that compilation on cards is by far the best method, and certainly this does achieve the greatest flexibility. If each reference is recorded on a card by itself, then the collection, when complete, may be arranged and rearranged as desired, so that each aspect may be brought out in turn. References dealing with lead in foods, for example, can be arranged first of all to bring together all discussion on the public health aspect, and then rearranged for methods of analysis, and so on. In compiling a bibliography, when each reference usually has to appear in only one place and when last-minute additions may occur, cards provide a most convenient method. They have two main disadvantages: first, the arrangement and rearrangement for different aspects can be a wearisome operation, and every card has to be looked at for every aspect; and second, since a pack of cards very soon becomes bulky, it is not easily portable, and in fact when the total passes about 250 some sort of container becomes necessary.

Much of the latter objection can be overcome by using paper slips or sheafs filed in ring binders. Each binder holds about 550 slips, a thickness of some two inches, as opposed to nearly six inches for the same number of cards. If there are many aspects to be dealt with, with continual rearrangement, sheafs do not stand up to handling as well as cards, but for compiling a bibliography, since they give nearly the same ease of insertion as cards and are much more portable, sheafs are probably the best method.

The other type of record, the loose-leaf book, lacks the flexibility of cards in the large sizes, where the page holds several references; in the small sizes, with one or two references to the page, it fulfils every requirement, for short bibliographies. Unfortunately the small ones hold only a limited number of pages, which can be a severe disadvantage, and may outweigh their advantages of ease of insertion, flexibility and portability. They can be constantly carried in the pocket and can also be fitted with tabbed alphabetical index leaves. For the survey of literature, the large sizes offer considerable advantages. Material on the various aspects of the subject can be collected together as compilation proceeds, by allocating new pages to each aspect as required, and entering relevant information from each article under each of the appropriate headings. Thus the same article may appear in several "chapters", and there is no need for any rearranging when the survey is actually being written, which not only saves times but is also a more certain means of including all relevant references when dealing with each aspect. Very little extra writing need be involved during compilation as it is not necessary to write out the complete reference each time. The "chapters" can be numbered and each reference given a sequence number within the chapter. Each article is then referenced in full in the first chapter in which it is noted, and in any other chapter is merely referred to by its chapter and sequence number.

This method retains a reasonable degree of flexibility in that each chapter can be extended as far as necessary, though within the chapters the sequence is fixed. Provided that there are not too many items in each chapter, however, this does not prove to be a great drawback, because the eye can easily take in a page more or less as a whole, and the classifying thus done during compilation eliminates much of the more mechanical part of writing the survey. In portability, the loose-leaf notebook is better than cards and about the same as sheafs, that is, it does not occupy a great deal of space in thickness, but the larger sizes—which are superior from the classifying aspect—cannot be carried in the pocket.

One of the most interesting aspects of a literature search is the way in which, during its course, one begins to obtain a more and more complete view of the subject. Librarians and information officers may often be asked to survey a field of which they know relatively little, and they do not therefore learn about it in the same way as the student. They may, indeed they probably should, begin with the latest publications, and the search itself takes them here and there with little regard for any normal time sequence. In passing, it may be remarked that this is also the way the researcher advances into the unknown. Under such circumstances, the most important factors are system and flexibility, system to keep track of what has so far been discovered, and flexibility to meet the inevitable modifications of viewpoint as the search proceeds. I myself find that the loose-leaf notebook meets these requirements so much better than any other form of record that I almost always use it. It is easier to look over what has already been recorded; new chapters can be added and relevant information extracted from the others in a moment; reference can easily be made both from and to other notes; and I dislike shuffling cards and still more sheafs. To me, the "infinite" flexibility of arrangement which these certainly possess brings with almost equally infinite weariness. But in this, as in other matters, each to his choice.

Usually, the enquirer himself makes clear the form in which he wants to receive his answer. As I have already remarked, no one in his senses would present a 50-page bibliography on metalworking to an accountant who merely wished to brush up his general knowledge of production methods. Sometimes, however, the nature of the enquiry, or the frequency with which it is received, makes it worth considering whether a permanent record of one sort or another would make a useful addition to the library stock.

Most author/title enquiries lead to the question of whether the document itself should be acquired, if not already in the library. If the same periodical has to be borrowed more than three or four times a year, it should be bought. For every article actually discovered to be of interest beforehand, several others usually turn out to contain useful information as well. A few articles that are worth copying, especially long ones, soon use up the cost of a subscription to most journals. Pamphlets may often be worth buying at once; they are usually cheap, and the location of a loan copy by the usual methods may present great difficulties, since the bibliographical control of what some librarians still happily refer to as "ephemeral material" lags far behind that for periodicals and books. Books are reasonably easy to borrow or obtain on approval so that the librarian and the subject experts can examine them before making a decision. The exception here is foreign books; technical books at least are often much more difficult to obtain than periodicals, of which specimens can nearly always be obtained by writing to the publishers.

Inter-lending of all kinds of material has increased enormously, and while the organized schemes of inter-lending are indispensable, it is well worth while building up a file of locations for material borrowed. Direct inter-lending between special libraries has also made great strides, and can often be quicker and cheaper than the official systems. Some librarians keep a special card index of such locations, and a file can also be built up quite easily by using the cancelled record of the original loan, if it has a suitable form.

Factual enquiries present a problem, in that the answer often comes from a source clearly indicated by the enquiry itself. No one would incorporate into their own indexes such factual answers as train times or specific properties of materials. Furthermore, enquiries of this type often arise out of special circumstances unlikely to recur. But where the answer has required a search, even a short one, it may be worth recording against a possible repetition, especially if the library maintains its own subject index, when all that is required is to file an entry in the appropriate place—the work of only a moment.

Subject enquiries of the kind that involve collecting data or actual documents should, I think, receive more systematic treatment, because the chances are that they arise from some continuing interest of the organization, so that their record may well have a more or less permanent value. Even where the enquirer himself does not ask for a bibliography or survey, therefore, the librarian should consider whether, having assembled the material, he might work on it himself and thus make a useful addition to his stock. This factor carries particular weight where the library has its own series of publications, which provides an appropriate vehicle and also passes on to all those on the mailing list the benefit of the library's work—again, a service of information of the highest value. I recall with pleasure writing a survey of a particular problem that had come up two or three times, because I felt it would probably be needed again and would make a convenient pamphlet to give to other research workers known to be interested in the subject. A few months later, a Government committee issued a somewhat controversial report that included some opinion on this particular subject, and my survey at once became in great demand and gave my colleagues some advantage in their discussions and meetings—an instance of how anticipation can help the library and one's own research colleagues.

An additional point in favour of such a bibliography or survey is that, being a separate document in its own right, it demands the proper treatment and is duly indexed and filed in the right place. As a member of a series, too, it may prove of the greatest value to others on the circulation list, of which the librarian never gets to hear.

In my book on *Assistance to Readers*, I devoted much space (too much, many people thought) to describing a form of record that had been found suitable for a particular set of circumstances commonly found in public libraries. In other types of library, I would also advocate a proper form for recording subject enquiries in the first place. This is not only because it provides a record that can ultimately be filed and indexed as a separate document itself, but also because one needs a working sheet on which to record information about the enquiry, the sources checked, the telephone calls made, and the final answer given. This serves the function of providing the librarian with an automatic memory, and also—a less vital point in special libraries, perhaps— enables the enquiry to be transferred from one member of the information staff to another with a minimum of time-consuming explanation.

The final question about records must be whether the record of an enquiry justifies itself by making a contribution to the reference service, and although this seems to call for powers of prophecy, the answer probably reflects the quality of the librarian's flair. So we come back to this indefinable attribute which carries us through the intricacies of reference service, and for which there is no substitute. But, as we have seen, these intricacies are of such complexity that flair has to be aided by system and method. Reference service is the information library's mode of existence, and both staff and readers profit when it can be orderly without sacrificing its inspiration.

FURTHER READING

Very little has been written on this aspect. The only complete work published in England is *The reference librarian*, edited by J. D. Stewart, published by Grafton, 1951, with a good chapter by Miss M. Exley on industrial libraries. Perhaps the best known general work is Margaret Hutchins' *Introduction to reference work*, Chicago, A.L.A., 1944.

Suggestions on technique are given by C. W. Hanson in his chapter in the Aslib *Handbook*, and:

A. D. Roberts: *Introduction to reference books.* Library Association, 2nd edition 1951.

P. Casimir: Enquiry techniques, in the 1955 RSL Conference Proceedings.

The American Chemical Society has published a collection of papers on *Searching the chemical literature* as Advances in Chemistry, No. 4, 1951.

CHAPTER SEVEN

Other Services

ACCEPTING the theory of the librarian and information officer's responsibility for the bibliographical preparedness of his organization creates at once an interest in several other techniques which have become quite a familiar part of the information library scene. Perhaps the most important of these is the translating of papers in foreign languages; indeed, a knowledge of several foreign languages is one of the qualifications suggested by Farradane for his "information scientist". On the other hand, there seems to be, for the present at any rate, fairly general agreement that a translator requires qualifications that are not necessarily part of the equipment of the information officer, who must, however, have some knowledge of the terminology of his subjects in as many foreign languages as possible. Without it he can scarcely carry out his obligations in the scrutiny of foreign journals—which should probably be done with even greater care than usual because the chances are that few of the research staff will have the time, or indeed the ability, to read them for themselves. Fortunately the abstracting journals give translated titles and summarize contents for many foreign papers, and incidentally provide quite a useful aid to the learning of special terminology.

Most of what needs to be said about translation in information work has already been said by B. C. Vickery, in an interesting and stimulating paper presented to the 1955 Conference of the Library Association. He pointed out the need for setting up national and international translating bureaux, so that research workers could retain their freedom to write in their mother tongue without thereby losing their opportunity of communicating with their colleagues in other countries. This solution appeals to me very much more than the more generally favoured idea of a new *lingua franca*—which would of course be English, which explains why the idea is the more generally favoured, since half the world's scientific papers are now written in English. How unreasonable of foreigners to expect to be able to write in their own tongues! But how great would be the outcry if it were suggested that the day of English might be passing, that in the future we might find ourselves obliged, in pursuit of the *lingua franca* ideal, to learn Russian or even Chinese! Of course knowledge of foreign languages will always be an enormously valuable qualification, especially, we may hope, as the national barriers erected by politicians begin to disappear, and research workers receive facilities for making contact with co-workers in all parts of the world. But this applies equally to the English-speaking nations, and is no reason why we should expect authors to *write* in a foreign language.

Already the regular translation of certain foreign scientific journals has begun, and no doubt the practice will spread, especially if the present high prices are reduced, as they should be, by increased sales. Meanwhile, the demand for translators in individual information services continues to grow as librarians and information officers cast their nets wider, which they must do to keep pace with the valuable work developing in countries that formerly may have done no research whatever. This demand is particularly noticeable in commercial information work where speed is so vital, and where so much information comes from press and other snippets that may very well remain for ever outside the scope of a national or international translating agency. But in technical and scientific fields also, it is often desirable to employ a translator for at least French and German, and it seems as if Russian will shortly become a desirable adjunct for every scientific information service. It is interesting to note here that the lack of emphasis on the production of consumer goods in the U.S.S.R. is reflected by the lower standard of the technical journals in these fields, as compared with the journals in science and basic technologies such as iron and steel or engineering.

The technique of translating involves much more than merely knowing the right words, and lies outside the scope of this book, except in so far as there is a similarity with information work itself. The basic qualification may well be in the languages and the techniques of translating, but obviously the greater the subject knowledge the better; and such subject knowledge can be quite well acquired on the job by a translator as by a librarian. Equally, a subject specialist with an interest in languages can turn his interest to good account by translating, and can widen his range of languages on the job. The difference is that, whereas the language scholar is following his chosen trade as a translator, the research worker has to cease practising his research while he is translating.

If centralized translating has not yet become the rule, considerable efforts have been made towards centralizing the indexing of translations already made, and the production of good technical dictionaries. Valuable work has been done in the latter sphere by Unesco, and continues to be done, by J. E. Holmstrom for example, whose own command of languages and range of subject knowledge make him approach the ideal of a technical translator! Several specialized foreign-language dictionaries have been published, and more would be welcome. Even short glossaries of highly specialized branches of science and industry are extremely useful, and, as in other spheres of information service, much has been achieved in this country by voluntary co-operation. Members of some of the Aslib subject groups have set a fine example to librarians in other fields, and it is of course in groups like these, with a limited and common interest, that co-operative translating is most likely to be successful.

It may be that my experience has not been typical, but I must admit to being sceptical of the value of centralized indexes of translations. The figures I have seen show that only a very low percentage of requests are actually satisfied, and few translations are used again. The scheme operated by Aslib may grow in value as years pass and the index becomes fuller; on the other hand, surveys of the use made of scientific literature suggest (as one would expect) that the chances of a particular paper being wanted tend to decrease fairly rapidly after about five years. Similarly, my view of the D.S.I.R. scheme for making translations may be coloured by the fact that nothing more was ever heard of my own requests, and Vickery reported delays of several months in 1955. I do not doubt that there are good reasons for these mishaps; but I cannot help feeling that they may possibly be inherent in the actual schemes so far operating or proposed.

Mechanical translating seems to offer a promising line of development, and a central translating agency equipped with such machines and producing "approximate" translations has more, perhaps, to commend it than any other form of mutual aid. Such machinery is costly to build and operate, but even a card index is by no means cheap—especially if it works at a low rate of efficiency. With a machine centre one would be sure of getting a result, and of getting it quickly. The editing and putting into exact English could be done by the library making the request, so that the centre would have less need to employ subject specialists able to cover every branch of research. Vickery gives examples of "machine English" which show that editing would not be a difficult or time-consuming labour for librarians familiar with their subject, and more recent examples show a considerable improvement.

What is quite certain is that librarians and information officers must actively participate in the many discussions now centering on this problem. Its importance, in science at least, may be judged by the fact that Vickery's paper received full-scale editorial treatment in *Nature*—a rare honour for a Library Association Conference paper. If we fail to express our decided interest, we may find that the ultimate form of organization established does not suit our needs particularly well.

This has already happened once. Microfilming has been known

for a hundred years, and has been a commonplace in commerce and industry for perhaps thirty or more. But readers and forms of microrecord really suitable for use in libraries are only now being produced by manufacturers, and this might have been delayed even longer had it not been for the devoted labours of a small number of people like Mrs Lucia Moholy, who for years made it a matter of principle to mention microfilm at every meeting she attended! It took a long time for manufacturers to realize that the needs of librarians were not necessarily the same as those of banks, export agencies and sales departments. Even now, it is the smaller firms in the industry that are seeking and benefiting from the collaboration of librarians.

There are three main forms of microrecord: roll film, film strip of various shapes and sizes ("microfiche"), and the opaque microcard originated by Fremont Rider. I think it is generally agreed that the last serves the purposes of libraries the best, that the microfiche is a reasonable alternative, and that roll film has so many disadvantages as to be perilously near to being a nuisance.

Nevertheless, roll film must unfortunately be bought because most makers produce it and because most readers are primarily designed for it. So we have the absurd situation of microrecords, which could provide so much research material cheaply for libraries, and save so much space, coming into use only very slowly because the predominating form is not particularly suitable, and because the standard type of reader involves dim lighting, ground glass screens, and mechanisms reminiscent of the horseless carriage. Add to this the final infliction, for the user, of having to go to the reader instead of having it brought to his desk, and then having the image planted straight in front of his face instead of in the natural position, on the desk at which he sits. Small wonder that librarians have noticed a reluctance on the part of research workers to use microfilm!

It is not necessary to dwell on the matter of unwinding and re-winding roll film; this feature has been improved on recent

94

models, and is actually used as a sales point, as if it were some striking advance to be able to do quickly something we would rather not do at all. The microfiche avoids it by putting few pages on each piece of film, which gives almost instantaneous location of any page. The attachment holding the fiche is usually a simple one; on the Dagmar reader, for example, it is held in position by magnets, one at each corner, a brilliantly simple idea. Originally, microfiche were lengths of only a few inches cut from roll film and containing a single row of frames, but this form, which was only used to any great extent on the Continent, is giving way to the "transparent microcard" described at length by L. J. van der Wolk and J. N. Tonnon in 1950, and now usually known as microfiche. I personally hope that this will supersede all other shapes and sizes for documentary records, and that the original single-row lengths will remain in use only for special purposes as "filmstrip" (or some such term already well-established). The great advantage of the 5 inch by 3 inch or 6 inch by 4 inch microfiche is that it can be filed in standard catalogue drawers; the use of white envelopes, cut away along the top front, keeps the film well-protected, makes it easily filed, and allows the title of the document to be read if printed full-size along the top of the fiche. An example was attached to the paper by Wolk and Tonnon.

There is no doubt, however, that the microcard proper, the opaque library-sized card, will be the main form in the future. After its invention by Rider, the microcard made steady progress in the U.S.A. because there were organizations willing to make them and reading apparatus for them. Some technical difficulties attend the construction of readers, because the cards, being opaque, have to be read by reflected, instead of transmitted, light. But these have now been overcome, and it is more than time that a good microcard reader became available in this country. Fortunately, research has been going on, and at least one firm, IOTA Services Ltd., hopes to produce a marketable microcard very shortly, and a reader to go with it.

95

Much thought has gone into the development of micro-records, and it is quite likely that considerable activity on both the publishing and the technical sides will burst upon us before long. Both Aslib and the Library Association have sub-committees studying the matter, so we may hope that when really steady progress is made here, it will be along lines favourable to librarians. Surely we ought to look forward to the day when cards and readers are cheap enough to enable scholars to collect their own cards and either buy their own readers as well, or have frequent use of one of the several that libraries will be able to afford. Already the Dagmar reader, an excellent small model, is sold in Holland at a special price to students. Small, portable readers with first-class technical qualities, and casting the image on the desk, used for compact, easily-handled microrecords such as cards and fiches; such a combination should go far, as Rider believed, to solve the problem of storage and ease of reference in libraries, and to give back to scholars the possibility of collecting their own libraries of texts essential to their research.

Another important service now commonly given by libraries is the provision, either gratis or at cost price, of photocopies, and it is interesting to see how, in this sphere, the most advanced information service marches side by side with the most "academic" libraries, even with the British Museum itself. The material copied may vary from a page of, say, the latest issue of the journal *Suisan Jijô Chôsa Geppô* (perhaps dealing with the canning of octopus), to the unique leaf of some ancient bestiary (perhaps describing a horrible sea serpent); but the technical problems are more or less the same, and from the librarian's standpoint the service is precisely the same.

To provide a research worker with a photocopy of a document he constantly needs takes a significant load off his shoulders, because he no longer has either to make frequent visits to the library, or to make a copy himself. It is generally recognized, in fact, that the service is vital to scholarship in all fields. With the introduction of cheap paper and apparatus, moreover, the practice has spread, and several libraries now prefer to copy material, if reasonably short, and give it to other libraries instead of lending the original. This has for some time been the custom in dealing with unique or rare works, but now it is often cheaper even with commonplace material, and has the same advantage of preserving the original. It is also, of course, a benefit to the borrowing library, which avoids the cost of returning the work and instead adds it to its own stock.

Information libraries benefit considerably, because so often the librarian borrows an article that he has seen in an abstract for the express purpose of copying it. If he gets a copy in the first place, he is saved even more trouble. This has been recognized by the Science Library in providing its photocopying service at a very cheap rate, and a similar service is available from many other libraries even though they do not operate a formal scheme. The Chemical Abstracts Service undertakes to supply a copy of any article abstracted if a copy can be located in the U.S.A., again at a very cheap rate.

All these services offered by the information library involve to a greater or lesser extent the question of copyright. Clearly, the rights of an author or publisher may be severely infringed if un-authorized copies of his work are scattered broadcast. In research, authors at least are usually only too anxious for their works to reach the widest possible audience, but some publishers now place a strict embargo on reproducing parts from any of their publications without written permission. The Royal Society, acting as a publisher, set a good example with its Fair Copying Declaration, which allows libraries to make single copies, for research purposes, of articles published in its journals, and many other societies and publishers have also subscribed to the Declaration. In fact, the practice of copying often benefits a journal by bringing it to the attention of a wider audience and so increasing its circulation.

However, as we know, copying in libraries is of sufficient importance to warrant the attention of legislators, and the 1956

Copyright Act has a word to say about it. Under the terms of the Act, non-profit-making libraries are permitted to make single copies, for research purposes, and not for sale except at cost price. This leaves us with the question of whether the libraries of industrial firms can be said to be "profit-making". In one sense, they make a profit for the firm even if it does not show in the balance sheet; in another sense, they cannot make a profit since they are not production units, unless they act as publishers and sell at a profit. It must also be remembered that the public and the university library are liable to be profit-making as they, too, supply readers with books which they turn to their own advantage, financial as well as intellectual. But the Act also states that libraries engaged in furthering scientific research may make single copies; and since this phrase is unqualified, it may, it would seem, be taken to apply to *any* library devoted to scientific research—and of this class the industrial libraries are among the élite. It is an interesting situation; but of one thing we may be certain, that if one is ever in doubt, the safest course is to seek permission. It is rarely withheld.

One day, we may devote a fraction of the energy and resources now concentrated on weapons of destruction to improving the communication of knowledge. Then, no doubt, all the present chaos in the publication and distribution of the results of research will be smoothed out. Until that time, the officer in charge of an information service must be alert to any new theoretical or technical development that may help him to keep his readers bibliographically prepared. I have mentioned a few points only in this chapter; but a new idea may turn up at any time, anywhere, and may be published in any one of many different forms. We need all the collaboration we can get, national and international; otherwise we shall fail in our job, and research itself will either slowly suffocate under the weight of publication or, more likely, groups of workers will restrict themselves more and more until free and open communication as we know it to-day ceases.

FURTHER READING

On translations, there is a very interesting book recently published by Unesco, edited by J. E. Holmstrom, *Scientific and
technical translating and other aspects of the language problem*, Paris,
1957. B. C. Vickery's paper was presented to the 1955 Library
Association Conference, Southport, and is in the *Proceedings*,
pp. 76-84; the comments in *Nature* appeared in the issue for
November 12, 1955, Vol. 176, No. 4490, p. 939.

A useful bibliography on documentary reproduction appeared in
Special Libraries, Vol. 48, No. 9, 1957; the whole issue carried
articles in reproduction and copyright, and the bibliography is
by no means limited to American material.

See also:

Fremont Rider: *The scholar and the future of the research library*,
New York, Hadham Press, 1944.

L. J. v. d. Wolk and J. N. Tonnon: "The microcopy on flat film
as an aid in documentation", *Review of Documentation*, Vol. 17,
Fasc. 5, 1950, and Fasc. 8, 1950; also issued as F.I.D. Publication
No. 257.

J. Burkett: *Microrecords in libraries*, Library Association, 1957.

Several articles by L. L. Ardern can be located through *Library
Science Abstracts*.

C. M. Lewis and W. H. Offenhauser: *Microrecording*, Inter-
science 1956.

CHAPTER EIGHT

The Educational Role of an Information Service

SO far, I have been dealing with the principal function of an information service, namely, the provision of information to experts. Another function could be developed, however: the provision of specialized material for non-experts, in aid of a more or less systematic course of instruction. As with the information service itself, the conditions existing in industry to-day are peculiarly favourable to this development, although it appears to be as yet in its infancy.

Similar services are given in other types of library; the university library owes its very existence to the need for books in courses of study as well as in specialized research work. But university libraries, while no doubt they have built up outstanding collections, lack the essential basis characteristic of the industrial library, its positive, continuous service, its responsibility for the bibliographical preparedness of its group. Similarly, in the public libraries, the Readers' "Advisory" service often plays an educational role in supplying specialized material to readers pursuing systematic courses of instruction. But the public libraries lack the community of interest with their readers which is so strong in industrial libraries and which makes it easy for industrial librarians to have a sympathetic understanding of their readers' needs; and, generally speaking, the staff of public libraries do not have the same detailed knowledge of the subject and its literature.

Earlier on, I questioned the desirability, and even the possibility, of evaluation by librarians or information officers for research workers. Evaluation has, however, a very definite part to play in educational work, because this class of reader chiefly requires help in selection. We are no longer considering service to research workers, and consequently the librarian is in a position to offer sound advice because it is based on his own practice in reference service and his contact with research; by these means he soon learns which publications are worth recommending and which are not. Through his own practice in writing bulletins and disseminating information he should be able to judge for himself which publications are worth recommending to non-experts for the manner in which their contents are presented.

So far as I can discover, little has been written on this aspect of information work, and this is certainly not because it is taken for granted. Yet it may well be that the very first industrial libraries had this function rather than that of serving research. The East India Company, for example, formed a library from which employees could learn something of the history of India and the conditions under which they might have to serve. The library of the New England mill described to the Society of Arts in 1855 contained books that would help the workpeople to learn about their trade. The Mechanics Institutions formed libraries, in the first place, so that their members could gain a technical education and fit themselves for the age of machinery ushered in by the Industrial Revolution; on their own level, they were the counterpart of the scientific societies and the great engineering institutions that were then coming into existence. In view of the persistence of the apprentice system, there must have been other libraries set up in factories primarily for educational purposes; indeed, the survey made by E. J. Rees for the 1922 Library Association Conference showed that a number of firms in South Wales did provide books for apprentices.

That these libraries did not grow into an organized movement, as research libraries have, may be deduced from two things: their absence from the contemporary scene, and the lack of literature about them. I find it impossible to believe that, if such a development had attained much significance, it would have died out, and not been written about. Works libraries, it would appear, have taken the same road the libraries of the Mechanics Institutions, and now serve principally, if not entirely, a recreational purpose. They have been completely overshadowed by the great development of research libraries, which aim to provide the expert with information that he can use in dealing with the problems allocated to him, but do not aim to provide the learner with what he needs to become an expert. Perhaps an exception should be made for scientists; many industrial research libraries do help young laboratory assistants to pass their examinations by supplying the textbooks they use in their classes. But important as this is, it is not the particular service that I wish to consider here.

Formal educational programmes in industry have expanded enormously since the end of the Second World War. Up to then, while there were plenty of apprentice training schemes, and educational facilities even up to degree standard were provided by some firms, there was nothing like the widespread interest that there is to-day. After the war, however, it became necessary to re-employ many thousands of men, now of mature years, who had been away from the technicalities of their work for several years; accordingly, short full-time "refresher" courses of instruction were provided. It is of interest to remember, in passing, that similar courses were set up for teachers, while those for librarians revolutionized our own professional education system and have remained as full-time Schools of Librarianship.

Sometimes these courses were arranged at technical colleges and similar institutions, but there were not nearly enough of them. Certain industries, then, and in particular those specialized industries for whom no technical college course was peculiarly suitable, began to supply their own needs by developing their educational programmes, first of all in order to deal with returning ex-Servicemen. The courses proved so successful that nowadays nearly every large firm has its own educational system, while Training Within Industry has achieved such status that it is universally spoken of by its initials only, as TWI.

Since the War, technical education has received an unprecedented amount of attention from all sides, and many national schemes are in force which enable younger workers to continue their education after leaving school, on a part-time and on a full-time basis. So widespread has the use of all these facilities become that the larger industrial firms nearly all employ highly qualified Education Officers with trained staff to initiate and co-ordinate further education. It is only in alliance with the Education Officer that the librarian can develop his educational work, and the first thing he has to do is to understand the nature of the further education that his new readers are receiving. An account of the various groups of trainees in one company was given by D. G. A. Sanders in a paper at the North-Western Polytechnic School of Librarianship in 1956, and while the pattern may obviously vary from one firm to another, the basic groups of employees remain similar enough to justify a brief general note here.

Beginning with the youngest, they may be divided into two groups: (1) those who, because the facilities exist, merely continue the study of subjects begun at school (including shorthand, typing, book-keeping, general knowledge), and (2) those who intend to pursue a systematic course of study leading to some professional qualification (including Associateship of the Library Association and similar bodies).

There are two main difficulties for the librarian in dealing with the first group. Firstly, they often remain a collection of individuals, each going off to his or her particular class at a Day Continuation College, for one day or more each week; and secondly, they often cease to attend these classes when attendance becomes a matter for their own initiative. In other words, they do not usually follow systematically and as a group a course of training in subjects likely to be covered by the firm's research library. The second group, on the other hand, do; consequently the librarian can easily demonstrate, if given the chance, the facilities that his library can offer them. Many firms go beyond sending their youngsters and apprentices to Day Continuation Colleges, and make use of sandwich courses, apprenticing to qualified and experienced senior workers, and full-time training centres established and run by the firm itself. If the librarian sets out to promote and maintain cordial relations with those in charge, the master craftsman or the head of the training school, he may be able to make the difference between the average, run-of-the-mill "hand", and the top class, forward-looking "engineer" who has acquired a thirst for information and knows where to get it.

Another group of students comprises more senior staff who have been selected to go on courses, in their speciality or in general subjects such as Management and Industrial Relations. In this category come also members of the information staff who may attend the short courses organized by Aslib, but these latter should have the advantage of being familiar with the use of the literature already. The librarian should try to ensure that he is informed of such courses, so that he can prepare the student beforehand with material leading up to the course and thus help him to derive the maximum profit from it. In this way, senior staff who may previously have thought of the library as either a luxury or as some obscure whim of the research department are brought to benefit directly from its work, and will more readily appreciate the follow-up after their course with more advanced and newly-published information.

Courses run within the firm by the Education Officer himself offer the best opportunity, because the subject material will be closely related to the firm's work and therefore to the literature in the library, and also because a visit to the research department by all the members of the course is often included. A talk on the use of technical information in the industry, and a visit to the library to get to know its resources at first hand, often stimulate some members to continued use afterwards. The librarian can increase the impact of the visit by offering to deal with enquiries arising out of the course or of any aspect of the students' work. I have found that confining the introductory remarks to a minimum, and using most of the time of the visit to let the students browse round the shelves, puts them at their ease and encourages enquiries. Furthermore, it is better to wait until the course is over before sending the answers or the literature required. For one thing, during the course students will have far too much other information to assimilate, and are not in actual contact with problems of their daily work. More important, psychologically, is that a personal letter to them at their place of work brings the library into contact with their normal routine, so that they come to regard it as an integral part of the firm's activities and not as merely a part of the training course.

This question of establishing contact may well be the most crucial. Research departments usually offer a striking contrast to production units in every way, and may seem to be surrounded by an atmosphere of mystery and remoteness. When this is allied to the deeply-rooted traditional feeling of superiority over book-learning felt by the practical man, the combination results in a formidable barrier between the librarian and his potential readers. It can only be overcome by bringing the library and its work into a direct relation with the daily work of the factory, and this is very far from being a simple matter. No progress will ever be made, for example, unless all the information staff make themselves thoroughly familiar with production processes; they should visit factories if possible, and mingle with factory staff at technical meetings (and, better still, on social occasions when no questions of seniority arise). Above all, the librarian should set up a line of communication from the library to the worker, either directly, or, as this may be difficult, through someone to whom the worker has direct access and to whom he is accustomed to turn for advice and assistance. Heads of Apprentice Training Schools, and Personnel Officers in factories, can often be enlisted as willing and indeed enthusiastic liaison officers.

It seems hardly necessary to add, but it is sometimes forgotten, that where a firm has a library in more than one department, the librarians gain a great deal by working in close collaboration, with regular meetings, like those held by the ICI librarians, to discuss problems arising out of the service, new techniques and new equipment. Exchange of specialized information is good for librarians as well as scientists.

I do not pretend that these few words account for industrial education. The point is that it has now become a recognized, indeed an integral, part of our industrial scene, a part that could not possibly be abandoned and which is likely to become more and more prominent. In a civilization that, willy-nilly, owes so much to the achievements of technology, any nation whose industry fails to improve the technical education of its workers is not only in danger of losing trade, but is also denying to its people the advantages they have a right to expect. Lest I should be accused of gross materialism, let me add that one advantage that I personally think we have a right to expect is greater leisure to enjoy the fruits of our education, more time for reading the poets and philosophers, for listening to concerts, for visiting museums and art galleries.

Here, then, in the educational programme, lies a splendid opportunity for the information staff. The existence of such a programme, like the existence of the research programme itself, means that the firm is prepared to invest in increasing the knowledge of its workers. It thus provides a system for the transfer of knowledge from one individual to another, and when people become conscious of ignorance they soon turn to books. Who can supply them better than the firm's library? I believe that the work demands to be done, and that it must be done by librarians. Furthermore, I believe that the virtual disappearance of the old works technical libraries resulted from the lack of anything like an educational programme. Any library service must grow out of a social context in which a need for information is felt; merely to put books on shelves and invite people to use them is not enough. The information service arose out of the formation of groups of specialists committed to acquiring information, the educational service arises out of the formation of groups of novices, but fundamentally the aim is the same: to increase the worker's efficiency and so make him a more valuable member of the organization—and indeed, of society.

FURTHER READING

I must reluctantly admit that the only articles I know on this subject are by me! North-Western Polytechnic, London: Occasional Paper No. 8, 1956, and *Library Association Record*, Vol. 59, No. 11, 1957, pp. 353-359.

CHAPTER NINE

Reports and Correspondence Registries

MANY Information Services do not include the correspondence registry of their organization, and this is understandable, because registries have traditionally been part of an office service, under the control of an office manager or even a typist. But their importance as sources of information has to be recognized, and there is now a distinct trend, in industrial research departments, to bring the registry within the Library and Information Service, where classification, indexing and circulation are well-understood techniques. Reference to any book on office management makes it clear that the problems facing the research registry are quite beyond the scope of what is usually recognized as "filing" by experts in office management.

It cannot too often be emphasized that an enquirer is, in nearly every case, completely indifferent as to the source of the answer to his enquiry, and it is particularly important that an organization's correspondence should be included in a search, because of its direct and continuous relevance to the organization's activities. If the files are kept separate from published documents, therefore, an enquirer has to remember to make his enquiry in two places, or he runs the risk of overlooking important information. The nature of the material probably makes it desirable to have a separate room for the registry, but serious consideration should be given to the possibility of including the information contained in it in the general information index, or at least locating the two indexes sufficiently closely together to make their connection obvious. Where the Registry is not a part of the Library and Information Service, arrangements should be made for at least the librarian to see all correspondence that contains new information. In some firms where this is the case, a copy of each outgoing letter is kept in the Library, and the new techniques of document copying make it possible to take off library copies of incoming correspondence as well.

This is obviously a somewhat inefficient procedure, since it involves building up two separate sets of more or less identical files, but it does ensure that the information staff are kept fully up-to-date with what is going on in the organization. It also avoids what would otherwise be very necessary, a search in two places for answers to enquiries.

If it is recognized, however, that as primary sources of information, correspondence files are just as important as other documents, the case for bringing them under the control of the librarian is clear. By this step, they will be given the technical processing normally given to library materials, that is, the recording of the documents and the indexing of their contents will be carried out thoroughly. I believe that organizations are beginning to realize that library methods applied to this kind of "current archive" material can make a useful contribution to their information resources; indeed, it is only by the use of these methods that the vast amount of information found in correspondence files, and often nowhere else, can be made available subsequently.

It follows, also, that a trained librarian should be in charge of this type of work and there are already several in industrial research departments. This trend will doubtless continue, particularly if these librarians build up a corpus of knowledge on new techniques of file control. One or two excellent reports have been published, but there is scope for a good deal of discussion and pooling of knowledge. There is as yet no familiar pattern, of the type that has developed in information services themselves, and of course the importance of correspondence files for retrospective searching can vary enormously in different kinds of organization. A scientific research department, like government offices, should have a strictly observed policy, while a commercial or service department may be able to discard all, or almost all, of its files after a few years.

Correspondence files are considered here as the records of the day-to-day life of an organization, but there is one form of record that is often treated separately and which has very definitely come within the purview of information services. This is the research report, which now presents problems of such vast and rapidly increasing dimensions that it has been given undue attention as compared with the equally important correspondence files. At the moment, confusion reigns in that no one really knows how to define a research report; the obvious definition, a document produced by a member of an organization to give the executives an account of what he has been doing, has been found unacceptable because of the practice adopted by some organizations of using the report form as a speedy but slipshod method of publication. Most (though by no means all) of these so-called "unpublished" reports begin as a record of work, and are therefore confidential to their organization, as with the United States Atomic Energy Commission, and some of the Research Associations. After a period, it is decided that the report need no longer be considered as confidential ("restricted"), and copies are therefore made available to other organizations.

The bibliographical control of these "unpublished" reports presents very great difficulties unless the issuing body sends them to a national bibliography; some of the Research Associations, for example, send their reports to the *British National Bibliography*, quoting a price, so that they are in effect acting as their own publishers. Far too many reports, however, become available only through personal contact. There are three main drawbacks to this procedure. Firstly, it is very difficult to get to know of the very existence of the reports; secondly, they are not obtainable from the usual sources, and ordering them has to be a departure from routine—a wasteful and expensive process; thirdly, and more insidiously, the mere widening of a report's circulation can mean unnecessary publication, because the report is often not pruned at the time, and the information it contains may be published again later in a journal, "to reach a wider audience". We are led inescapably to the conclusion that on the one hand information is often lost to those who could use it, while on the other hand much information is circulated more than once, so swelling unnecessarily the already mountainous sea of publications.

Within an organization, however, reports can be closely controlled, and they are often considered as part of the library stock; some librarians, in fact, are responsible for editing and issuing, as well as recording reports. This is highly desirable, since it means that the librarians can benefit from their own experience as users of reports, and ensure that their productions are at least bibliographically sound. The primary requisite for a report is an unmistakable identity, which usually takes the form of a serial number; there is also everything to be said for adopting a standard format, which ensures that the author's name, the title and the date are given prominence. It means a slight extra production cost, but this is negligible compared with the time saved in using the report. A characteristic appearance can also be a ready means of identifying the issuing department, and most organizations regularly producing reports have now adopted standard formats and layouts. Several large books have already been published on the writing and production of reports, and this is some indication of the importance that they have now assumed.

Most writers, however, take it for granted that reports will be treated as completely separate items, and doubtless this is usually true. For one thing, it is much easier; all that is involved is to give each report a number, file them in a separate sequence, and keep proper indexes. If there are not too many, a simple list in serial number order may be enough, though it soon becomes a very tedious business finding a report whose number is unknown. A list in serial number sequence for each author can be a very useful aid, and is not expensive to maintain. Quite often an enquirer remembers that the piece of work he wants was done by a particular author; or he may want all the reports written by an author; or an author may want copies of all his own reports. The last contingency can sometimes be avoided by the usual practice of giving authors copies of their reports at the time of issuing, but while most research workers are careful to keep a file of reprints of their published work, they are not always so systematic about the reports they write for restricted circulation.

Author and number indexes are certainly useful, but it must be recognized that a subject index is essential if the file of reports is frequently consulted. If the reports are in classified sequence, an alphabetical subject key is sufficient; if the reports are in serial number sequence, as is usual, a classified index with an alphabetical subject key should be maintained. For while numbers are scarcely ever remembered, and authors' names, however reluctantly we may admit it, are also easily forgotten, the one thing that is certain to be remembered is the subject, or part of the subject. In fact, if a specific report is asked for, it is because it deals with a particular subject: reports are not often read for their literary or sentimental value.

The reason why it is so important for reports to be accessible by subject is of course because the work of any research organization continues on the basis of what has already been done. Even when entirely new projects begin, as a first step the researcher assembles all the knowledge already available in the department; and indeed this is one of the reasons for the importance of libraries in modern research. Reference is constantly necessary to report files because organizations are interested in research on *subjects*, and it is usually, though not always, unprofitable to do the same work twice. Thus when a research worker asks for reports, he does so because he thinks that there may be information in them relevant to his current programme, and it often happens that such information is contained in a report dealing mainly with some other subject.

It is clear from this that reports are not the only documents likely to contain information relevant to a research programme: reports may constitute the formal research record of an organization, but they are not the whole of the record. Many other types of document also form part of it; letters, minutes of meetings, notes of telephone calls and all the miscellaneous assortment of papers that go to make up a correspondence file.

In a research organization, such files are as much part of the record of the organization's work as its formal reports, because they arise naturally and inevitably out of the progress of a research project. When a researcher wishes to read the history of a project, therefore, the file will certainly be useful to him, as well as the reports. In fact, if reports are sent to other departments, as often happens, they are likely to provoke correspondence themselves. It therefore seems logical to file a copy of a report with the correspondence relating to the project. It may be desirable to keep other sequences of reports, by number or by author, according to the use made of them, but a copy in the file will certainly be useful. If this practice is not followed, there should be in the file a reference to all relevant reports and a summary of their conclusions.

Some groups of files present no problem of arrangement, because they are built round a "name"—a customer or a supplier, for example. Some writers on office management, in fact, suppose "Name of correspondent" to be the only conceivable factor by which files can be arranged. This way of arranging certain files undoubtedly serves the user's purpose better than any other; but the subject files of a research organization are best arranged in a systematic, classified order. This makes a great deal of work, of course, and some librarians who have studied the problem do not advocate classified order; one firm even goes so far as to arrange all its letters in a single sequence, with good indexes, on the hypothesis that all, or very nearly all, enquiries are really for single letters, even though the enquirer may actually ask for all the correspondence dealing with a particular subject. This is certainly an original view of the matter, and should not be dismissed on the same grounds as we would nowadays dismiss the idea of an unclassified library of books. It is safe to say that the problems of organizing materials of this kind are far more complex than those that arise with the easily handled, compact book, which makes it all the more regrettable that so little attention has been given to them in the Aslib *Handbook of Special Librarianship*.

My own view, however, is that a classified arrangement is likely to be more helpful most of the time. Admittedly, many enquiries can be resolved into a request for a single letter, but even so, the other relevant documents will almost certainly be of some use. No one should be expected to carry in his head the history of what may well be a very large number of research projects, and a file for each provides, if properly maintained, a mechanical memory of much greater efficiency than a human memory.

The decision to adopt a classified sequence brings its own difficulties, because it poses at once the question of what system of classification to adopt. Attempts have been made to use the UDC, but the classifying of very specific research projects results in extremely long numbers. The effect of this can be—indeed usually is—grossly overrated; those who are accustomed to using UDC are not unduly distressed by such numbers, and if a classification is to be *expressive* of subjects (as it must be to be of any use), those accustomed to scientific thinking readily appreciate that a many-faceted subject requires a more or less lengthy notation. Nevertheless, the UDC notation, being an attempt to reconcile enumerative and faceted classification, soon becomes much too long for easy identification. For files, moreover, there is an additional reason for wanting a short notation: it can be used for quoting as a reference in correspondence. An overworked typist will be unwilling to add to her burden by typing out long sequences of numbers at the head of her letters, especially as absolute accuracy is so necessary.

Probably, therefore, a special classification system will have to be devised to suit the special needs of each organization. Before the principles of constructing a faceted classification were known, this was a formidable task, and though not so formidable as making a system for published literature, because of the limitation in subject coverage, it usually provided a sufficient deterrent to the adoption of a really systematic scheme of classification. But now that the construction of a faceted scheme has been described in reasonable detail, the task has been made much easier, and I have no doubt that, once this method becomes well known, and librarians have gained experience in using it, it will provide a most valuable tool for organizing correspondence files.

Reports on their own present no peculiar difficulties in classifying and indexing, beyond those that arise through the very precise nature of their subjects. Correspondence files, on the other hand, pose some very interesting problems in addition to those normally associated with library materials.

First of all, the file itself must be adequately indexed according to its subject, or "Name of Correspondent"; a detailed name index, in fact, is essential, not only for "Name of Correspondent" files themselves, but also for names of organizations and important individuals associated with the subject files. For the subject index, the "chain procedure" that goes with a faceted classification will provide the main headings necessary for each file. Both of these indexes are commonplace in library practice. There are, however, other important aspects of indexing files, arising mainly from the fact that a file, unlike most library materials, is a growing thing; only when the project is completed do the contents finally cease to grow. Some projects never reach completion, and their files have to be arbitrarily divided into chronological periods.

In classifying and indexing books, it is the subject of the whole book that is treated, and apart from analytical entries for subordinate subjects treated in major parts of the book, no attempt is made to index all the information contained in it. Usually, an index to the book itself is provided at the end of the text. In indexing correspondence files, both of these types of index have to be provided: the index of file subjects, and the index of file contents. This means that extremely elaborate analytical indexing has to be done, and accounts for the practice, in some registries, of indexing every single letter. The problem arises: should the indexes be combined in one, or should the index of contents be attached to the file itself, on the analogy of the index to a book?

It is very difficult, and may not even be very desirable, to give a definite answer one way or the other; both methods are certainly practised with success. On the whole, it seems to me that, since the registry staff themselves are compiling all the documents that relate to the organization of their files, they would be well advised to keep the number of *separate* records as low as possible; as we have already seen, recording takes up a good deal of the time of registry staff. This would mean combining the subject index and the contents index in a single sequence of subjects, and, it should be pointed out, does not save any time in compiling records. It should, however, save time in consulting them, since the user obtains a more accurate reference from the index; if he is seeking a precise piece of information, he should not have to note a subject reference, and "browse" through the individual contents indexes to perhaps more than one file before he finds exactly what he is looking for.

Analytical index entries should always be clearly distinguished from main subject entries if they are filed in the same sequence, and there are several well-known ways of doing this: coloured cards, different coloured inks, or a special form of words and layout. If a classified sequence of cards is kept as well as the sequence of files, analytical entry cards can be filed behind the main subject card, if there is one, for the same subject, and the same alphabetical subject index card will do for both. If no classified sequence of cards is kept, the analytical entry must be shown either on the alphabetical subject index card, or on another card next to it and distinguished from it in some way. Of these two methods, the first is probably better; not much has to be written on a subject index card, so it is not likely to become crowded with words, and it reduces the number of places in which the user has to look—so also reducing the danger of not looking there at all.

Another awkward feature of correspondence files that can create great confusion if not strictly controlled is their habit of changing their subject—not completely, of course, but sufficiently to make the connection obscure and therefore hard to remember, and, what is more important in a classified sequence, sufficiently to alter the place of the file on the shelves. This can be illustrated by the file which starts as an examination of a particular method of solving a problem, or the use of a particular material for some purpose; both fail, or fail partially, and an alternative or modification is tried. Sometimes, it occurs that the method or material is by chance discovered to have some other use than the one investigated. When this happens, the original file can be terminated, and a new one begun—that is, if the point of change is perceptible, which is not always so. This means that if the research worker needs the whole case history, for a meeting for instance, he has to use two files, but this is not an enormous disadvantage, and is perhaps compensated by the gain in precision of reference. An alternative is to re-classify the file at a broader heading that will contain both old and new subjects. In either case it would be desirable to link the two subjects by means of a reference in the index: a "see also" reference for the first alternative, a "see" reference for the second.

In an organization of any size, where individuals of more than one section may be engaged on the same project, the circulation of files is essential, and a means of recording the whereabouts of files must be adopted. If the circumstances permit, the loans system in use in the library can be used; the advantage is that the users do not have to become familiar with two systems, and they treat all library materials with the same respect—especially when it is explained to them that the system infallibly indicates the borrower and is accepted by the management as doing so!

Cavalier treatment of library and registry property is not unknown, and should never be tolerated.

The main requirements of a loan and circulation record are that it should be quick in operation when issuing files, and quick in revealing the whereabouts of a particular file when it is asked for. It may, in some circumstances, also be desirable to keep a chronological record of loans, and even a record of loans under borrowers' names—in other words, the loans records usually kept for books. Many different systems are in use, but all of them are based on the same principle: that of using a form of record (a card, a slip, a loose-leaf ledger, a bound ledger, etc.) to stand in place of the file, and keeping as many sequences as are necessary to meet the conditions required. One advantage that can be taken of the nature of files is that one copy of the loan record can be placed in the file's own position, standing where the file normally stands. This means that there is only one place to look when the file is asked for, as even if it is out on loan, the loan record will be there to show who has it.

One rule in circulation is wisely observed, but sometimes not easily enforced: each time a user sends a file forward to another user for attention, it should be routed via the registry in order that the transfer can be recorded. Where a formal messenger service exists, the problem does not arise, because a messenger can just as easily take a file to the registry as to another office. But where typists are the means of communication, and in particular where one typist serves both first and second user, it is not so easy to ensure that the proper record is kept of a transfer. Files are so valuable that some registry superintendents insist on a signature for every file issued; this makes a deal of extra work, of course, but it does provide incontrovertible proof of possession. Personally, I have never quite been able to accept the necessity of such a procedure: it does not, after all, of itself bring back a file that has been lost, and no one can really make up the loss, which is all that matters. It may make users more careful, but it seems to be a tiresome and time-consuming precaution against a loss that occurs only rarely, that should not occur at all, and that cannot be replaced anyway.

Each organization probably has to make its own rules for discarding, but as a basis the best guide is without doubt the Public Record Office Pamphlet issued for the instruction of government offices. For the purposes of most industrial firms, this may be too cautious, since it bears the responsibility of keeping up the national archives. Firms, on the other hand, need keep only what they think will be of lasting value to themselves, though many are now giving more attention to their archives on behalf of economic historians. A research department has to keep most of its files for a considerable time, because they constitute a record of work that is very likely to retain its value, while a commercial department may well be able to discard everything after no more than a few years.

While discarding policy should be decided by each organization for itself, some standard procedures can be adopted for carrying it out, and perhaps the most important is that both policy and procedure should be written out and used as a manual by the staff. It is very easy to look on discarding as a minor facet of registry work, and to do it as and when the spirit moves. But this can soon result in confusion: overgrown files, with all their extra opportunities for loss and damage, dead files lumbering up valuable space, index cards referring to work no longer current, extra registry equipment needed; all these are in direct opposition to the basic principles of registry operation—ease and speed—and following a well compiled manual of procedure should prevent them all.

The chief decision required is what to discard, that is, what is no longer required in current use, what may be transferred to storage as "archives", and what may safely be destroyed. Some types of document clearly fall into each of these categories; so much so, that in some organizations they are marked with a symbol designating the appropriate category as soon as they are received. One firm, for example, marks ephemeral papers with a "T" (for Temporary) in the top right hand corner, in order that papers so marked can be taken from the file by a junior clerk after the necessary time interval. This is a very useful practice; the superintendent or chief clerk has to see all papers on receipt, but if a satisfactory system of marking like this can be devised, he does not have to spend time in weeding the files as well. Nevertheless, the necessity for caution must be emphasized: it is so easy to destroy papers that do not appear to have any future interest, but impossible to be sure that one's decision is right. I recall an instance where a printed card acknowledging receipt of a letter (receipt being confirmed in a subsequent letter) was later wanted for the name of the man signing it!

There are two basic ways of carrying out discarding: as a special operation, or as a continuous process. Each has its advantages, but in large registries the two begin to merge into one another. Where most of the material no longer in current use has to be kept, as in research departments, the continuous process is probably better, because the papers are subjected to further treatment, as archives, and are not simply thrown away. Where most of the material can safely be thrown away, the special operation method has the obvious advantage of giving more psychological satisfaction. Papers have so much less appearance of value than books that the chance to destroy large piles does not bring even the faintest pang of regret to any but the most miserly registry assistants. This actually is important, because it means that the task is less distasteful, and might indeed be welcome; consequently it will be done thoroughly.

Until quite recently, most registries used the standard four-drawer filing cabinets for housing their files, with or without suspended pockets in which to place the individual files. This method has certain outstanding disadvantages, as is well known, and is by no means cheap. But it seems pointless to discuss it here, since I believe that it is rapidly disappearing and is most unlikely to be used by any new registry. The new systems of suspended filing on shelves are now available from any of the main office furniture suppliers, and are decidedly superior. They are cheaper, make better use of floor space, and are easier and quicker to use. The shelves can be obtained with dust blinds or with lockable doors and one or the other is desirable, according to circumstances.

The siting of registries is an interesting question, since, like libraries, they are used by many people who do not make them their actual place of work. It is important, therefore, that they should be situated as conveniently as possible, and for large organizations, decentralization according to the departments served is usually recommended by organization and methods experts. Decentralization has two advantages: it divides the files into small and easily-managed groups, and it brings these groups near to those who use them. Dividing of files into such groups has indeed everything to recommend it—provided that any necessary links between groups are maintained. When all the groups are housed together in one registry, this is done by the index. But if the groups themselves are housed in different places —if the registry is divided up, that is—this necessary linkage will be difficult to achieve without a central index. By all means decentralize, therefore, but let each small registry send copies of its index cards to a central index; the gain in co-ordinating information will more than offset the labour of compiling the index.

A file is a case history, and so has an internal unity and cohesion. But no part of an organization's life exists in isolation, and files reflect this interdependance of parts and projects; it often happens that the same document will be of use in more than one file, and copies have to be made. The importance of these records for current use has long been recognized, and their value as sources of reference in research is becoming increasingly obvious. The application of good library techniques is absolutely essential to the operation of registries, but while there is a considerable body of experience in existence, it is not reflected in the literature. It is to be hoped that the demand will stimulate some of those who have this experience to make it available to others by writing and publication.

FURTHER READING

There are several books, mainly American, on writing technical reports, but one of the oldest and most respected is British:

Sir Clifford Allbutt: *Notes on the composition of scientific papers*, Macmillan, 3rd edition, 1923.

A recent comprehensive American work which deals with organization and all aspects is:

B. H. Weil, editor: *The technical report*, Reinhold, 1954.

A very good general work on correspondence and unpublished papers is:

J. E. Holmstrom: *Facts, files and action*, Vol. II, *Filing, indexing and circulation*, Chapman and Hall, 1953.

Two useful papers, by D. V. Arnold and Miss E. W. Parker, appeared in *Aslib Proceedings*, Vol. 1, No. 3, 1949, pp. 235-250.

On discarding, the best guide, if naturally inclined to caution, is the pamphlet issued by the Public Record Office, *Principles governing the elimination of ephemeral or unimportant papers in public or private archives*, which has also been printed in Chapter 3 of Ronald Staveley's *Government information and the research worker*, published by the Library Association in 1952.

Also edited by Staveley and published by the Library Association is *Unpublished report material*, 1957.

CHAPTER TEN

Training and Qualification for Information Work

WE come now to the most vexed question in the whole of information work—one, indeed, that the Aslib *Handbook* chooses to ignore: what are the appropriate forms of training and qualification for the staff of information services? There has been a very great deal of argument over these, and I fear that no answers acceptable to all parties have yet been found. My experience in serving on a joint committee of Aslib and the Library Association leads me to believe, reluctantly, that no such answers exist, because two irreconcilable points of view are in conflict. My own opinion, which I should state at the outset, is that the profession of librarian and information officer is one, and that its members use the same types of materials and techniques in pursuit of the same end. Furthermore, I am strongly opposed to the view maintained by one faction, that there is some characteristic peculiar to *scientific* literature that distinguishes it from the literature of other subjects, so requiring a separate profession of *scientific* information officer, or information *scientist*. Those who worked in a particular organization as scientists, and changed over to work on documents, have every reason to value their qualifications and experience, and to be proud of the contributions they have made to our profession. But the man with an economics degree who spends his time selling is a salesman, not an economist, and the man with a history degree who designs buildings is an architect, not a historian. A. B. Agard Evans summed up the matter characteristically, at the 20th Aslib Conference in 1945, when he referred to the "elementary but fundamental error in trying to distinguish between a special librarian and an information or intelligence officer. They were precisely the same animal, whatever the local term".

I shall try to analyse the position briefly, putting down the tangible things characterising the work and the profession. I use the word "tangible" in contra-distinction to J. E. Farradane, who makes much of such things as one's "approach" or attitude of mind to a subject or technique, but does not specify how such a thing could ever be a matter for professional training and qualification; it is, in fact, almost entirely a matter of individual personality.

Strangely enough, when we come down to brass tacks in the matter of desirable educational standards and qualifications for information staff, little disagreement arises. No one would pretend that subject knowledge is unnecessary, and the more the better. All are agreed that some knowledge of the techniques of librarianship is necessary, since "information officers" (in the context referred to in this book, at any rate) administer libraries; there is some controversy over the emphasis to be placed on various aspects of librarianship, but we may all admit the need for variety and alternative choices in the syllabus. In this book, I insist on the need to have a working (even if sketchy) knowledge of as many foreign languages as possible, for here is one's chance to help research colleagues who do not have such knowledge. In order to produce literature surveys of real value, an ability to write clear and attractive English is essential. And probably the most important qualification of all is not one of knowledge, but of character: a sympathetic understanding of the way a research man works, and patience to pursue even the most elusive bits of information, however wearisome the search.

These qualifications are not easily gained, and rightly so, since a profession in which honours are won cheaply has itself little value. I think we may agree that a new entrant to the profession would be unlikely to possess them all, and professional education of some sort is therefore desirable. The main conflict of opinion arises over what pre-entry qualification should be required, and what a course of professional education should cover; from this disagreement arises the third, and fundamental, issue, namely, what is the appropriate body to provide certification.

Let us consider the four major types of qualification I have mentioned, beginning with subject knowledge. It used to be maintained—in fact this was one of the main points advanced on behalf of the "information scientist"—that a science degree was an absolute minimum and that this clearly ruled out nearly all qualified librarians. The issue was as simple as that. And without any doubt a science degree is a most valuable asset in information work, as in many other professions. The argument against this "absolute minimum" was that a degree course is not the only way of learning a subject, and that as most information services covered a far wider array of subjects than any degree course does, even a science graduate would still have to go on acquiring subject knowledge. This is particularly true nowadays owing to the great increase in specialization of university studies.

Recently, however, the partisans of the "scientist" camp have been caught on the horns of a dilemma, and have had to give away their position. When commercial research work began its energetic and valuable development, under the label "information", it differed so clearly from commercial librarianship that some scientific information officers eagerly seized it as a powerful reinforcement of their argument that the *content* of information work differs from librarianship. Unfortunately this claim rebounded. In the first place, the commercial research workers hastened to dissociate themselves from their new allies in the most uncompromising terms! Their work, they said, was quite different in content from that of the scientific information officers, and would remain so. Nothing, therefore, was gained, though a pretence is still kept up. In the second place, the claim to unity between scientific and commercial work implied, and indeed was intended to imply, that scientific information officers were capable, by virtue of their membership of this new profession, of carrying out commercial information work. It was evidently not appreciated at the time that this claim destroys the previous position of requiring a degree in the subject. One or two half-hearted gestures have been made to try to retrieve the position: Farradane, for example, tried to compromise in his discussion of the scope of information work by saying that "If economics is counted as a science, this included the business man who requires economic information". But in general the matter is hushed up as much as possible, and it will be interesting to see how far the scope of "science" extends now an Institute of Information Scientists is established.

A further point that must be emphasized is that the manner of selecting heads and assistants for information services has changed. I have already described how usually, in the beginning, a scientist already employed by the organization moved from the laboratory to the library section when the need made itself felt, and very often he stayed with the same organization for the whole of his career. Conscious of the value of his subject knowledge, it was only natural that he should think that it was an indispensable pre-requisite for any kind of information work. Nowadays there is a very strong trend towards the advertising of even the highest posts, as almost any issue of *Aslib Proceedings* shows. In other words, there is developing that freedom of movement, from one organization to another, that is one of the characteristics of a profession. But if we consider that this is desirable, as indeed I do, then we have to accept a lesser emphasis on subject knowledge, and realize that such knowledge can quite properly be acquired on the job.

To avoid misunderstanding, I should like to end this part of the discussion by stating categorically that I do not by any means minimize the value of subject knowledge; on the contrary, I am sure that it must be either possessed or acquired. Neither do I belittle the possession of a degree; this, too, I think to be desirable, and the closer the subject to the work of the organization, the better. What I do not believe is that both or either of these things are at the same time unnecessary for librarians. Some information officers, in their zeal for making the distinction, actually reach the ultimate futility of maintaining that, doubtless because of some unspecified biological handicap, librarians *cannot* acquire subject knowledge—even librarians with a science degree! Personally, I am quite convinced that, however hotly it may be denied, this is because they consider "librarians" to be the young ladies who carry out the clerical operations necessary in a library; only that and nothing more. In industry, one is constantly meeting this opinion; it stems largely from the fact that, in the public library, it is usually the junior assistants that one meets most frequently. But this view is changing, even if it is still nourished in some diehard bosoms.

One of the reasons for the change is the growing respect for the professional side of the work, which, by a happy irony, arises mainly from the efforts of information officers themselves. For a long time the banner of librarianship was carried in this country by public librarians, but the initiative has largely passed from them since the war. This is not at all a criticism, but almost a law of nature, that a rapidly developing organism is likely to have more vitality, to throw off more sparks, than an old and well-established one. We should, in a properly organized profession, be mutually helpful and not mutually suspicious.

In the matter of professional qualification and certification, it is obvious that the Library Association, with its Royal Charter, should be the authority. Unfortunately, if the Association sowed the wind by ignoring what was new in information work in the early days and by its calculated policy of scorn and suspicion ever since, it has certainly reaped the whirlwind since the war. Time and again efforts have been made to set up a distinctive qualification for information work, and they continue; years of discussion lead to deadlock. It may even be that Farradane was right: "It is perhaps possible that the librarians might have risen to the opportunity; if so, they missed the boat!"

However, this is only true of the past; and representatives of moderate opinion on both sides have made strenuous efforts latterly to reach an agreed form of syllabus for examinations that would be suitable "for both librarians and information officers". In this book, I have tried to give an outline of the scope of information work as I understand it, and, with the exception of technical details such as binding, storing and mechanical aids, I believe I have covered every aspect of what is commonly accepted as information service. I have left out public relations, liaison work and other functions that are sometimes allied to information service; similarly, I have left out teaching, textbook writing and other functions on which even librarians can be demonstrated to engage without making them part of librarianship. I have, in fact, covered much the same ground as the Aslib *Handbook*, because it represents the only standard we have to judge the contents of activities specifically labelled "Information Work", presumably with the acquiescence of the "scientific" party.

Now, with one exception to which I attach great importance, these contents are already in the syllabus of the Library Association's examinations. If it remains a question of "attitude" or "approach"—a thing impossible to examine out of a specific context—surely the sensible thing is to co-operate in running the teaching and examining and so contributing valuable knowledge and experience to professional education? Some information officers refuse to do either; some, among them Mr Farradane, have put us in their debt by contributing valuable lectures to the teaching courses; and some regularly give whole courses specifically directed towards the Library Association examinations. Indeed, a few librarians actually lecture to courses run by Aslib for Information Officers! Valuable co-operation already exists, in fact, on a large scale.

The important exception is that part of an information service that is concerned with the presentation and dissemination of information, mainly dealt with in Chapter Five. For several years I have been of the opinion that criticism by information officers is justified so long as this remains outside the syllabus. It is demonstrably an integral part of the work of an information library, and of most other types of library also, even if only to a limited extent. A sub-committee of the Reference and Special Libraries

Section of the Library Association gave long and detailed consideration to the matter some years ago, and arrived at a syllabus for such a paper. This was forwarded to the Library Association for consideration, with the suggestion that the appropriate place might be Part 4 of the Final Examination, where it would take its place alongside other special options such as Palaeography and Archives.

This paper was not considered until 1957 because it was hoped, and expected by most people, that there would be a favourable outcome to the negotiations carried on by the joint committee of Aslib and the Library Association, set up at Aslib's request following an overwhelming vote, at the Aslib Conference in 1953, in favour of a unified system of examinations. When these negotiations unfortunately broke down, the Section again pressed for the introduction of its paper, and this will be done in 1959, after a statutory period of two years to allow teaching bodies to prepare courses.

The proposed paper covers methods of disseminating information, and also presentation. It therefore includes another talent required for information work, the ability to write clearly. This is a matter that has received a great deal of attention recently, particularly in science. Some writers, especially in American engineering journals, have plumbed the depths in their desperate attempts to achieve clarity and simplicity. Discussions in this country have remained on a reasonably scholarly level, partly because there is already a long and respectable tradition of study in the subject, and partly because much of the recent stimulus has come from the Presentation of Technical Information Discussion Group, which was formed at University College, London, after the series of lectures by Professor R. O. Kapp, in which he put forward his idea of "Functional English" for the writing of technical and scientific papers.

The last of the four qualifications is a knowledge of foreign languages, and in view of the main requirement of knowing the terminology of a limited field in many languages, a university degree in languages would not necessarily be the best start, especially as most of such courses concentrate on the literary side. For information officers (who are not professional translators) it seems likely that this particular skill is best acquired on the job, where one can concentrate on the material actually received. On the other hand, there is no reason why language graduates should not take up information work (apart from full-time translating) if they are interested in research in specialized subjects, and they should be able to take the new terminology in their stride, though this would be harder in scientific than in commercial research.

Of the four main types of qualification, therefore, all are certificated in some way. What distinctively characterizes a profession, however, is the combination of the material worked on and the work done on it. Hence the value of professional experience, about which I have said nothing so far, because each individual has to acquire his own in his own way, even though he may benefit from that of others as well. It has been suggested that registration of information officers might be on a basis of degrees, Library Association examinations, and experience. I cannot see the value of a qualification based largely or entirely on those issued by other bodies. Whenever a suggested syllabus is published for a special examination, however, the compilers seem unable to wrench it very far away from the one already operated by the Library Association. We come back to the same question: is not co-operation preferable to fragmentation, in a profession so small as ours?

If the information officers who adopt the "separatist" standpoint seem to be the chief target of attack here, it is not because they are solely or even chiefly responsible for the split in the profession. It is inevitable that qualified men should value their own qualifications more highly than those of other people, especially when they have spent years demonstrating the advantages of their qualifications in their chosen profession. Furthermore, we cannot shut our eyes to the fact that most of the teaching and examining for Library Association examinations has been done by public librarians for many years, and since the system serves them reasonably well, they are reluctant to change it. Several years as a member of the Library Association Council have shown me how deeply rooted is the notion that a "library" is by definition owned and operated by a local authority, and I recall more than one assistant, full of the greatest promise, who abandoned courses for the examinations because the lecturers were incapable of dealing with any but public library matters. In certain circles, it is regrettably still true that public library practice is regarded as the desirable norm, and others as aberrations.

But in educational thought at least there has been considerable progress during recent years. The Schools of Librarianship are forging steadily ahead, and seem to be quite united in their determination to teach librarianship, not one particular variety; they give their students the opportunity to visit and work in libraries of all kinds. As more information librarians qualify as Fellows of the Library Association, they become eligible to serve as examiners. As I have already noted, many distinguished information officers now co-operate by lecturing in both full and part-time courses. All the necessary preparation for complete co-operation has been done, and it will be a grave misfortune for the profession if those representing the extremes of opinion on each side cannot be persuaded to come to a compromise. If they will, there seems to me to be no reason why the profession should not reach its cherished aim of an academic standing equal to that of any other.

FURTHER READING

Three good papers appeared in *Current Problems* 1956, the Proceedings of the RSL Conference, by W. B. Paton, J. E. Farradane, and J. C. Harrison. Farradane and Leslie Wilson give the "information officer" viewpoint in the *Communications* of the International Congress of Libraries and Documentation Centres, Brussels, 1955, Vol. IIB, pp. 76-81 and 94-96. The Library School view was also given at Brussels, by

Roy Stokes, Vol. IIB, pp. 85-90. My own opinion on "The graduate in librarianship" appeared in the *Library Association Record*, Vol. 57, No. 6, 1955, pp. 213-218.

The American scene is surveyed in *The training of literature chemists*, published by the American Chemical Society as Advances in Chemistry No. 17, 1956.

CHAPTER ELEVEN

Further Developments in Information Service

THE temptation to prophesy what might happen for the best in the future is well-nigh irresistible, and it so happens that this is a particularly auspicious moment for prophecy in our profession. Several promising developments are already under way, and with the Roberts Committee reporting on public libraries to the Minister of Education, and the International Conference on Scientific Information in Washington in November 1958, we may expect many more important proposals to come forward during the next few years.

Pride of place, as far as scientific information services are concerned, goes to the National Lending Library for Science and Technology. Salvaged, as it were, from the ruins of the South Bank scheme, the plans have gone ahead well during the last two years, as Dr D. J. Urquhart, who is at present directing the project, has reported. We cannot yet form any clear idea of the extent of its future impact; but one thing is certain, that it will greatly increase the range of the world's scientific literature that is available to the individual information library. And as anyone who has surveyed our resources in the literature of any subject knows full well, there is plenty of scope for improvement as far as foreign works are concerned.

If we believe that the special libraries are now the vanguard of the profession, it seems logical to consider how much their characteristic contributions can be adapted to suit other types of libraries. The first steps have already been taken, with the organizing of several local schemes of co-operation, beginning with the famous and now veteran Sheffield Interchange Organization, now fashionably known as SINTO. This and the schemes recently established in Liverpool, LADSIRLAC, and Hull, are based on large city library systems, and industrial firms are invited to co-operate. We are all familiar with the great contribution that SINTO has made over more than 25 years to industrial development in the Sheffield area, and it is already clear that the others have made their mark and will develop rapidly. A new scheme based on technical college libraries, is being organized by Hertfordshire County Library.

A scheme of a different kind is CICRIS, which is not based on a single large library, but on ten libraries in the West London area which have joined in a co-operative venture with its headquarters at Acton. R. D. Rates, who was the prime mover and first Secretary of CICRIS, read a paper on it to the Reference and Special Libraries Section Conference in 1956, and the Conference put forward a resolution urging the Library Association to help to establish similar schemes in other suitable areas. As a result, some discussions have been held, and the possibilities of two areas, Newcastle-on-Tyne and Reading, considered. Attention has first been focussed on Newcastle, rather fortunately, it would appear, in view of the recent publication of the Curtis Report on provision of technical literature in that area. It is hoped that preparations for a scheme will be completed there in 1958.

These are not by any means the only schemes of co-operation, though they are probably the most highly organized interlinking of special libraries with public and college libraries. Each is making its own special contribution. SINTO began as a means for co-operative provision of periodicals, and has published a large number of first-class technical bibliographies; CICRIS has a well-developed system of subject specialization, and has compiled union lists of periodicals, foreign language dictionaries, commercial and scientific reference books; LADSIRLAC has gone a stage further in emulating the special library and regularly produces a Documents Bulletin.

As an example of a similar development in the university field, and in a field outside science moreover, we may point to the co-operative efforts of the librarians of university Institutes of Education. Although all save one of these Institutes came into existence only after the war, they have succeeded to a high degree in helping each other by exchanges, inter-lending, specialization, and the compilation of the *Index to Selected British Educational Periodicals*. This is at present circulated only to the Institutes, but the possibility of wider distribution is under investigation.

These, and other similar schemes, are means by which libraries join together in order to improve the services they can offer to their readers. When we turn to the individual library's service, it is hard to escape the conclusion that nothing like the industrial information service at its best can be developed in other types of library so long as the proportion of staff to readers remains so low. Farradane has estimated that a first-class information service needs something like one to every ten qualified research workers—remembering that each qualified worker implies two or three of the supporting arms, laboratory assistants, typists, cleaners and so on. Since the information service demands a close and continuous contact between staff and readers, it would be difficult to achieve in large cities, for all readers, or even within the more limited circles in universities.

This is no reason why we should not make the attempt. Much has already been done in public libraries to develop common interests with groups of readers, through local societies, youth clubs, schools; some libraries keep a classified index of readers' interests, and notify them of new publications that they might like to see. The Guildhall Library has set a splendid example of how to exploit its stock through its own publications, with the *CRR Courier* and the *Guildhall Miscellany*. It may be expected that other librarians will follow this lead, and the impact a concerted effort would have on scholarship might surpass all our hopes, because there is no doubt a wealth of interesting material in our public libraries. The *Manchester Review*, of course, is well established, but is not quite the same because of its predominantly "library" interest, and shows how well articles on professional topics can be linked up with material appealing to a wider audience.

A line of approach that has always seemed to me to be full of promise and yet strangely neglected is an information service by the public library to the staff of its own Town Hall. This is given in some places, but I do not know of any library that has systematically developed such a service to a high level. It seems strange, because local government matters must be well within the interest of most active public librarians, and an appreciative Town Hall staff would surely prove powerful allies in times of crisis, when budgets are liable to be cut.

A step of this kind has to be taken with the utmost circumspection. Even scientists are sometimes reluctant to admit that they know less about the literature (though more about the subject) than their librarian and information officer. But since they have appointed him to be their watchdog, they expect him to attract their attention at appropriate times. Experts in a subject have to be handled very tactfully by a librarian wishing to offer them an information service. This is particularly true of universities, where the academic staff often pride themselves on being authorities on both the subject and its literature. Luckily, Bradford's Law of Scattering, which seems to operate in every field, comes to our assistance, and the best way to open negotiations is perhaps to take along an article bound to interest the reader but published in a journal he would never think of consulting. From such small beginnings as these spring all our information services.

In the future, then, I expect the methods of special library information services to become more or less a part of the methods of all other types of libraries. The closer relationship thus formed between libraries should help to unify the profession, and may be encouraged by the work of the Roberts Committee. This committee resulted from a White Paper, and was set up by Lord Hailsham when Minister of Education. It has to consider the whole structure of the public library service, in relation to local government organization, and also in relation to other types of libraries. Those of us who have attended Library Association Conferences are well aware that such discussions on professional matters are always liable to come under the influence of the parish pump, but whatever happens, the report of the Roberts Committee will be a most important document for libraries of all types.

Of greater importance for the information library is the International Conference on Scientific Information scheduled for November 1958 in Washington. It is sponsored by the National Academy of Sciences-National Research Council, the National Science Foundation, and the American Documentation Institute, and is pursuing lines of enquiry similar to those of the Royal Society Scientific Information Conference of 1948. The Conference is being limited to about 150 participants, in order to ensure a high level of discussion, and is organized in seven groups:

(1) Requirements of scientists for scientific literature and reference services.
(2) Function and effectiveness of abstracting and indexing services for storage and retrieval of scientific information.
(3) Effectiveness of scientific monographs, compendia, and specialized information centres for storage and retrieval of scientific information.
(4), (5) and (6) Organization of information for storage and retrospective search:
  (4) comparative characteristics of existing systems;
  (5) conceptual and mechanical problems in the design of new systems;
  (6) possible development of a general theory of storage and search.
(7) Responsibilities of governmental bodies, professional societies, universities, and scientific and industrial organizations for research and training in scientific documentation and for operation of scientific information services.

The Royal Society has set up a committee to co-ordinate British representation, and several British librarians and information officers have been asked to submit papers.

So we have come full circle: once again science appears as the driving force behind new developments in information service, and there is no need to underline the potential value of this Conference for librarians. One point, however, does seem to merit special attention, and I have already referred to it in previous chapters. At the 1948 Conference of the Royal Society, J. D. Bernal put forward a proposal for reorganizing the publication of results. During the Conference, Bernal withdrew his proposals because of the opposition they aroused among editors, who suspected (without much reason) an attack on their autonomy. But as Dr R. S. Cahn, editor of the *Journal of the Chemical Society*, said in his paper to the 1955 IUPAC Conference on the Documentation of Applied Chemistry:

> J. D. Bernal ... already in 1948 ... proposed that papers should be submitted to a central agency who should classify and disseminate them to those who asked for papers on individual topics. ...
>
> Bernal's proposal was certainly premature, but it is not too early now to begin thinking of the position as it will be, say, 10-20 years hence. When that time comes journals will be twice their present size, relatively few Fellows will pay for them, and industry and the State will consider whether their subsidies which will have become burdensome are really necessary: whether some better means of recording and distributing scientific results cannot be found.

The IUPAC Conference was disappointing in some ways, especially in that it was not particularly productive of results. But unless the Washington Conference pays some attention to the organization of publishing and the decrease of overlapping and repetition, we may find ourselves in an impossible position in another ten years. If the *Chemical Abstracts* index for 1947-1956 fills 19 volumes, what will be its size for 1957-1966? Let us not forget that one result of the IUPAC Conference was that, since 1956, *Chemical Abstracts* has increased its coverage significantly by copying from the *Referativny Zhurnal*! It is absolutely imperative that the alarm should be sounded as often and as loudly as possible at Washington.

This is the third conference of its kind since the war, which proves beyond question the importance of information services in the world to-day. If the emphasis in this book has been on science and technology, it is because this is the field where new developments have been most remarkable. But, as I have said, it is not only in science that information services are wanted; the pressure of publication falls on all research workers, and if we desire the continuous extension of education and research, we must be prepared for the consequences: more publication still, more need for libraries. The whole object of research is to increase man's knowledge of himself and his environment, and in pursuit of this aim every research worker has the need, and the right, to communicate with his fellow-workers.

Libraries occupy a central position in the process of communication, and in information service we recognize that our role in the transmission of knowledge must be active and not passive. It may well be that the librarians who for so long collected and preserved documents secured the foundations of our civilization. We, in our turn, by the collection and dissemination of knowledge, have our own contribution to make towards the building of the future.

Index